DEC 0 5 2

#52
Sun Valley Branch Library
7935 Vineland Avenue
Sun Valley, CA 91352

P9-DNG-473

Your
Left-handed
Child

hamlyn

DEC 0 5 2008

Your
Left-handed
Child

Making things easy
for left-handers in
a right-handed world

370.1543
M661

1830

16873

Lauren Milsom

An Hachette Livre UK Company

First published in Great Britain in 2008 by Hamlyn,
a division of Octopus Publishing Group Ltd
2–4 Heron Quays, London E14 4JP
www.octopusbooks.co.uk

Copyright © Octopus Publishing Group Ltd 2008
Text copyright © Lauren Milsom 2008

Distributed in the United States and Canada by
Sterling Publishing Co., Inc.
387 Park Avenue South, New York, NY 10016-8810

All rights reserved. No part of this work may be
reproduced or utilized in any form or by any means,
electronic or mechanical, including photocopying,
recording or by any information storage and retrieval
system, without the prior written permission of
the publisher.

Lauren Milsom asserts the moral right to be identified
as the author of this work

ISBN 978-0-600-61480-7

A CIP catalogue record for this book is available from
the British Library

Printed and bound in China

10 9 8 7 6 5 4 3 2 1

Contents

Foreword

My husband Keith and I are both left-handed, and together we have spent the last 18 years working with other left-handers, researching and raising awareness of their needs through the Left-Handers' Association. We also commission and provide left-handed equipment through our specialist retail website, anythingleft-handed.co.uk.

For over 30 years, our family ran the first ever left-handed shop – the famous Left-Handed Shop in central London – and welcomed visitors from all over the world before rising costs forced us to close our doors in 2006. Now, we are delighted to say, we reach those same customers and many more through the pages of our website, and our Left-Handers' Club boasts over 50,000 members – all immensely proud to be left-handed. (For information about the Left-Handers' Club, see page 121.)

We are also parents of a left-handed son and a right-handed daughter, so have experienced at first hand the hurdles a left-handed child has to overcome at school and home. Over the years we have been fascinated to witness the vast improvements in learning that can be achieved by employing more creative study techniques that appeal to 'right-brain' thinkers.

If you are a right-hander caring for a left-handed child, you have no doubt already discovered how giving early guidance in even the simplest

A left-hander's good spatial awareness gives her an advantage.

Allow your child to choose whichever hand works best for everyday tasks.

everyday activities such as dressing, feeding, painting, cutting and baking can be very awkward (and messy!) when approached from the wrong position. Having a right-handed daughter has made me acutely aware of the awkwardness of being opposite-handed to one of your children – in our family the left-handers are in the majority and we have had to learn to accommodate the sole right-hander in our midst!

Often a subtle change can be remarkably effective, and the strategies and suggestions set out in this book are simple but effective, having

been tried and tested among many families worldwide over many years. It is important to remember that not all left-handers are the same, even in the same family. Be mindful of possible difficulties that may arise but do not assume them, or make your child feel unnecessarily aware of handedness. Being sympathetic to individual needs, and where necessary providing solutions to specific problems in a relaxed and encouraging manner will ensure your child is confident and capable, and that left-handedness need never become an issue.

Introduction

Introduction

As a parent you will no doubt have invested a great deal of time and effort studying all aspects of childcare and child development, made decisions on a healthy diet for your child, the best games to help him develop, and ways to encourage his social and emotional development. Yet few of us give any thought to one of the most important aspects of every child's make-up – his handedness.

Getting to grips with left-handedness

As your left-handed child grows, you are responsible for making his journey through life a happy, safe and rewarding one in a world that is largely inconsiderate of his needs. By educating yourself about handedness, you will be able to determine the strength of your child's hand preference, dispel the myths and preconceptions surrounding left-handers, and give him the confidence and skills to approach tasks in a safe, comfortable and effective way that will enable him to fulfil his potential.

If your child is the first left-hander in your family, you may be surprised to learn that left-handers are actually quite common. Latest figures suggest that approximately 13 per cent of the population are naturally left-handed, irrespective of social pressures or acceptance.

Born a leftie

Left-handedness is a trait we are born with. Because of many different cultural superstitions regarding left-handedness, this trait has historically had rather negative connotations. In many cultures, left-handers have been treated with suspicion or even ostracized from society, with left-handed children forcibly made to conform to right-handed actions such as writing and eating. Not surprisingly, such cruel practices not only hindered left-handers' ability, making them appear awkward and clumsy through

Try it yourself

If you are right-handed yourself, try going about your daily life using your *left* hand to work tools and equipment and to complete and guide your tasks.

Next time you pick up your normal, right-handed household scissors, put them in your left hand and try to cut out a simple shape accurately – you are automatically pushing the blades apart, and the top blade is covering the cutting line, so don't be surprised that the end result is torn and uneven – and that your thumb knuckle hurts.

Now try cutting a slice of bread with your usual serrated bread knife, but use it in the left hand. The doorstep wedge you create isn't due to your incompetence, but because the knife is serrated on the wrong side for left-hand cutting.

You will soon see how awkward it is, and realize that our world is set up for right-handers' convenience. This means that left-handers have to do most tasks back-to-front, and with equipment that is not designed to work for them.

Involve your child in the layout of his room, desk and play area so that everything is within easy reach.

undertaking everyday tasks with their weaker hand, but also created poor self-esteem and even psychological damage, which could last a lifetime. We now understand how damaging such attitudes are, and thankfully they are dying out in most civilized cultures. They are also futile, as it is impossible to change a person's natural dominance and, while living in a society that does not accept left-handedness can force people to use their non-preferred hand for tasks, it does not stop them being more adept with their natural hand, nor from being 'right-brain thinkers'.

Rising to the challenge

After years of working with and talking to left-handers, I am firmly convinced that this very fact of living in a world where even the simplest actions can present a challenge because of right-biased designs and layouts can actually be one of a left-hander's greatest strengths.

Your child's early years are a time of exploration and new experiences, and much of the value a left-handed child derives from your care is the chance to learn how to adapt to a right-handed environment. This adaptability is one of the greatest advantages left-handers have over right-handers, who never have to solve the problems that left-handers encounter on a regular basis. What you can do is provide your child with the encouragement, suggestions and confidence to approach potential obstacles as challenges, and explore together the possible solutions.

In this book you will find details of the most common challenges that your child will face, together with lots of simple and useful strategies to overcome many of these day-to-day obstacles, making life more comfortable and efficient for your left-handed child, and instilling him with the confidence to approach these difficulties with a positive attitude.

Adapt or compromise?

One big advantage your child will have through being left-handed is that of learning to be very adaptable, making right-handed layouts work wherever possible, and in the most efficient way. Throughout this book you will find suggestions for the most efficient ways to adapt to a right-handed environment, so that by the time he is a teenager your child will have learned to cope with most situations, hopefully taking left-handedness so much for granted that it is never an issue.

The lip on this milk pan is the wrong side for a left-hander, forcing him to pour backwards.

However, there are many instances when there is no efficient or comfortable way to adapt, often when using tools and equipment with a definite right-handed bias. In a typical day there are many situations where left-handers have to compromise – using tools or working in situations that are awkward, uncomfortable and in some cases actually dangerous.

Most right-handers simply do not understand this, and why should they? Unless they have a left-hander in their immediate family, they probably have no idea of the range of tasks that can present left-handers with difficulties. More surprising, however, are the number of left-handers who are oblivious to the inequality all around them, and the additional inconveniences they are put to every day. This is because, having adopted a style of using a tool that makes it work (however awkward it may appear) the action is regularly repeated and becomes normal. Since they cannot compare the action to that of a right-hander, they are totally unaware how much easier and comfortable the action is when performed right-handed.

It is only when presented with a properly designed left-handed version to use that left-handers can experience the comfort and efficiency that right-handers experience every day! Since left-handed versions of everyday tools and equipment are rarely available in mainstream stores, left-handers are denied the luxury of comparison between right- and left-handed versions, and so the ignorance is perpetuated, and the struggle continues.

When left-handers first use fully left-handed utensils, they realize that they have not actually been adapting, but compromising in hundreds of small ways in their daily lives. They are surprised to find that within a few short minutes of using a left-handed tool they have easily adjusted their style of use, and drop the sometimes awkward manner they unconsciously adopt to make the right-handed versions work. It is no surprise that the most common criticism we left-handers face is that we are 'awkward' and 'clumsy' at some tasks. What right-handers don't appreciate is that we look that way because the tools we have to use are back to front!

A wonky cut, scissors that tear and awkward can openers and peelers are all the result of right-handed design.

A creative bent

It is likely that your little left-hander will be highly creative – not just in traditional arts and crafts, but also in ideas and perceptions of the world. It is no coincidence that the great artist and inventor Leonardo da Vinci was a left-hander, or that there are a far higher than average number of left-handed architects.

Left-handers are right-brain thinkers (see Chapter 1, pages 18–19), good at seeing and manipulating images in their mind. This, coupled with an ability to think laterally can make them excellent and innovative problem solvers, who will often be able to see a solution to a problem that others may not have recognized. Your left-hander may bring a refreshingly different viewpoint to your family, and who knows – may even broaden your own horizons!

Much has been made of the high proportion of left-handers among the high achievers in society, and it has to be said that there are some very talented and remarkable left-handers throughout history and in the world today. Could it be that a natural propensity for lateral thinking, used on a daily basis to overcome everyday problems, enables left-handers to solve greater challenges in later life? Or is it an innate creativity?

Whether, as is often claimed, left-handers make up a proportionally higher number of successful people than among the population in general, particularly in the arts, music and sport, is very hard to calculate. Nevertheless it is inspiring to see the contribution left-handers have made to our lives and culture.

Jimi Hendrix

Bill Gates

‘ Being left-handed is not a disability or a disadvantage. It is simply a difference. Respect your child's difference, accommodate it where necessary, and always celebrate it. It is part of what makes her the person she is. ’

Famous left-handers

Henry Ford – car manufacturer
Bill Gates – founder of Microsoft
Matt Groening – cartoonist, co-creator of Bart Simpson (also left-handed!)
Bill Bryson – author
Alexander the Great – Greek hero and conqueror
Julius Caesar – Roman emperor
Robert De Niro – actor
Kurt Cobain – singer
Bob Geldof – singer
Ronald Reagan – actor and former US president
Bill Clinton – former US president
George Bush Sr – former US president
Jim Henson – creator of *The Muppets* and *Sesame Street*
Buzz Aldrin – astronaut
Angelina Jolie – actress
Nicole Kidman – actress
Tom Stoppard – playwright
Fred Astaire – dancer and actor
Charlie Chaplin – actor

Hans Holbein – artist
Leonardo da Vinci – artist
M.C. Escher – artist
Michelangelo – artist
Mark Twain – author
Lewis Carroll – author
Jean Paul Gaultier – fashion designer
Bob Dylan – songwriter, musician
Noel Gallagher – songwriter, musician
Damon Albarn – songwriter, musician
Jimi Hendrix – musician, guitarist
Paul McCartney – songwriter, musician
Ringo Starr – drummer, singer
Paul Simon – songwriter, musician
Greta Garbo – actress
Babe Ruth – baseball player
Martina Navratilova – tennis player
Brian Lara – cricketer

You can find a huge list of famous and high-achieving left-handers on the anythingleft-handed website. (See Resources, pages 122–123).

Martina Navratilova

Julius Caesar

Development of Left-handedness

All in the mind?

The brain is key to every aspect of our body and mind, from muscular coordination to interpreting what our eyes see to the way we figure out problems. The control of movement and senses is 'cross wired', so that, put simply, the right side of the brain controls the left side of the body and vice versa.

Left brain, right brain

For many years people considered that, in addition to controlling the left side of the body, it was the right hemisphere of the brain that was responsible for visual concepts, spatial awareness and perceptual thinking. This naturally led to the assumption that right-brain attributes would dominate in any mental or physical activity left-handers undertook. This is a theory that has been enshrined in folklore, with people being classified as either 'logical' left-brainers or 'creative' right-brain types.

In reality the interaction between the two sides of our brain is far more complex than that, with all of us drawing on the skills located in various parts of our brain all the time, and the two halves communicating and interacting constantly via a bundle of communicating nerves called the *Corpus callosum.*

This is not a book on the complexities of research and studies into handedness, and the debate still rages as to the influence our handedness has over our talents and abilities.

However, my experience with left-handers, together with numerous studies we have undertaken, does seem to suggest a strong leaning towards creative and artistic interests. Many left-handers choose careers in media, arts, music, information technology and architecture, where a talent for visual and spatial thinking is essential. The preference for one hand over the other, particularly for intricate tasks, is a signal as to the way our brain is wired. Through a person's handedness, it is possible to surmise many of their strengths, natural talents and skills.

The language centres

Language is thought to be strongly linked with handedness. The language centres are located in the left hemisphere in the majority of right-handed people (95 per cent), whereas in a significant minority of left-handed people (30 per cent) the language centre is either located in the right hemisphere or partially located in both hemispheres (see illustration on page 19).

Communication

The *Corpus callosum* links the two hemispheres of the brain, and allows communication between the two.

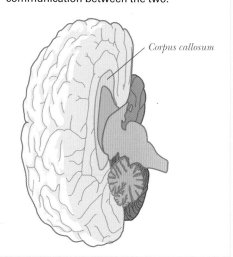

Corpus callosum

Traditional roles associated with the two halves of the brain

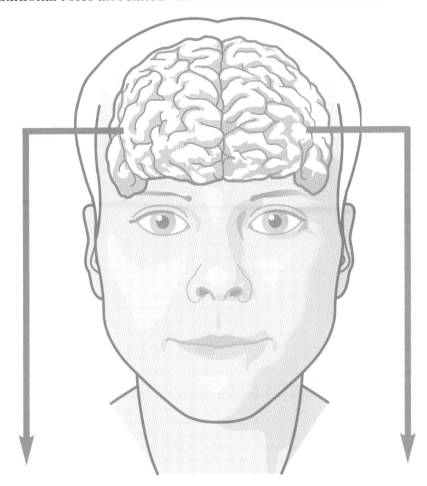

The right hemisphere (**left-hand control**) controls the following functions:

- Movement in left side of the body
- Visual concepts
- Spatial awareness
- Perception
- Creativity
- Emotions
- Attention
- Musical aptitude (melodic)
- Pitch and intonation
- Art
- Inspiration
- Language

The left hemisphere (**right-hand control**) controls the following functions:

- Movement in right side of the body
- Speech
- Language
- Writing
- Logic
- Analytical thought (mathematics, science)
- Complex rhythm
- Sequence
- Linearity
- Lists

Theories about left-handedness

Nearly everyone has some preference for using one hand or the other for certain tasks (lateral preference), and over the years there has been a great deal of speculation and research on the causes of handedness. Although none of these have yet proved conclusive, it is widely thought that left-handedness is inherited. It certainly does seem to run in families, although not in a predictable way.

Genetic (natural) left-handers

Research into the genetic cause of left-handedness is very popular, with many research teams trying to identify a specific gene for handedness in humans. Most recently, an international group of scientists, led by a team from the Wellcome Trust Centre for Human Genetics at Oxford University, have identified a gene that they suspect modifies the development of asymmetry in the brain, increasing an individual's chance of being left-handed.

A genetic link does seem to be borne out by statistics. Where one or both parents are left-handed, there is a higher chance that they will have a left-handed child. One of the most recent and comprehensive studies on the genetic basis of left-handedness, by Dr Chris McManus at Oxford University, has been detailed in his fascinating book on handedness, *Right Hand, Left Hand* (see Resources, pages 122–123). His analysis of survey data showed that around 9 per cent of children of two right-handed parents will be left-handed, as will 26 per cent of children born to two left-handed parents and 19 per cent of children with one left- and one right-handed parent, slightly higher if it is the mother who is left-handed (see box below left).

Dr McManus believes there is a genetic pattern for right-handedness, which would always make offspring right-handed, and a variable gene pattern that, if inherited, has an equal chance of making us right- or left-handed, a bit like tossing a coin – if it lands one side the child will be right-handed, and on the other, left-handed. This would explain why families can have a mixture of handedness among their children, even though

Left or right?

- Two right-handed parents have a 9.5 per cent chance of having a left-handed child.

- One right-handed and one left-handed parent have a 19.5 per cent chance of having a left-handed child. (The chances are higher if it is the mother who is left-handed.)

- Two left-handed parents have a 26.1 per cent chance of having a left-handed child.

Signs that your child may be a pathological left-hander

Early signs to look for are:

- Favouring the left hand very strongly from a very early age (grasping, thumb sucking etc.)

- Restriction of growth in one hand or foot

- Very poor right-hand skills.

Your child may choose his left hand for intricate tasks long before he starts writing.

both parents may be right-handed, and why it is not possible to predict handedness in the same way as, say, eye colour.

It would also explain why identical twins often have different handedness, despite sharing the same genetic make-up. According to Professor Stanley Coren in his research at the University of British Columbia, about 1 in 5 pairs of identical twins have discordant handedness – one being left- and one being right-handed. Although this seems a very persuasive theory and does help to explain some of the anomalies between parental handedness and that of their children, more research into the subject needs to be done to settle the matter conclusively.

The chances of having a left-hander in the family increase the more children you have (that is, the probability of, say, a couple's third child being left-handed is higher than for their first child). So there is still hope for right-handed parents – if you have enough children, you may still be lucky enough to have a left-hander!

There is often a genetic history of left-handedness in a family, but this can be hard to trace.

Pathological (forced) left-handers

The human brain has a wonderful ability to compensate for injury, and in some instances is able to retrain parts of the brain to take over tasks another area can no longer perform – a phenomenon often seen in stroke victims who regain use of faculties lost during the stroke.

The rather scary term 'pathological left-hander' relates to a theory that might explain the small proportion of left-handers who have no genetic link to other left-handers in their ancestry. It simply means that the child is left-handed because of some injury or stress (however slight) that occurred to the brain early in life, possibly before, during or shortly after birth. The child would have been right-handed but for some injury, either permanent or temporary, to the left hemisphere, which induced a shift dominance to

the non-affected side. Problems such as birth stress (such as prolonged labour, premature birth, breech birth, Caesarean or multiple births, and forceps delivery), haemorrhage or anoxia (deficiency of oxygen) are common forms of damage that occur at this time in development.

The motor fibres descending from the *left* cerebral cortex affect the motor movement of the *right* side of the body (lower arm, hands and fingers, lower leg, some of the eye muscles and tongue). If the damage occurs on the left side of the brain, the child may have a weaker right side. Severe damage may result in cerebral palsy or hemiplegia (paralysis) on the right side of her body but in the case of much smaller damage the brain may compensate by shifting language and motor dominance over to the right side of the brain, resulting in left-handedness in what would otherwise have been a right-handed child.

Sometimes these children experience additional problems or learning difficulties, which may be why we hear about higher than average percentages of left- or mixed-handers among dyslexics, ADHD sufferers and other learning disabilities. This is not always the case however, and despite the unfortunate title, it is quite possible for 'pathological' left-handers to show only very minor evidence of impairment, and often none at all.

A forgotten past

Trying to determine whether a child is a pathological left-hander is not always straightforward. Just because your immediate family doesn't include any left-handers, do not automatically assume your child's left-hand preference is pathological. Genetic left-handers do not necessarily appear in every generation, and your great great-grandmother, for example, may have been left-handed, but if forced to use her right hand by social convention of the time, her natural handedness may have been hidden and forgotten about. The likelihood of having a left-handed child not only varies according to the handedness of the parents, but also according to whether there is any genetic history of left-handedness further back up the family line.

Facts and figures

- More than 50 per cent of left-handers do not know of any other left-hander anywhere in their living family.

- Around 75 per cent of left-handers have two right-handed parents and only 2 per cent have two left-handed parents. (Although the probability of a left-handed couple having a left-handed child is more than double that for a right-handed couple, left-handed couples only make up about 1 per cent of the population, so have a tiny percentage of the total left-handed children.)

- On average, between 7 and 8 out of 10 children born to two left-handed parents will be right-handed.

These figures are supported by surveys quoted in Professor McManus's book and also by surveys undertaken among members of the Left-Handers' Club (see page 121).

If your baby constantly feeds herself with her left hand, she may well be left-handed.

Degrees of handedness

There is a broad spectrum of hand preferences in human beings, ranging from those who strongly favour one hand or the other for all one-handed tasks to the truly ambidextrous, who can do all actions (including writing) with either hand equally well.

Left, right or mixed?

Generally speaking, a left-hander is defined as someone who writes with the left hand, since this is one of the most intricate and precise skills we perform and is the best indicator of our fine motor skill development and hand–coordination.

Researchers usually classify left-handers as those who answer yes to the following:

- Do you use the left hand to write?
- Is your left hand preferred for the majority of key tasks?
- Is your left the most skilful, proficient or most able hand? (This can be measured by manual single-handed tasks comparing the use of one hand then the other, such as timed peg moving on a peg board.)

The hand we write with does not necessarily mean we use it to the exclusion of the other. Many left-handed writers prefer the right hand for different tasks, just as there are people who write with their right hand but are comfortable using their left hand for a number of tasks (mixed-handers). Only about 1 per cent of the population is able to write equally well with both hands.

This idea of strong and mixed-handedness has recently promoted quite a lot of scientific interest, with a number of research studies focusing more on the benefits or otherwise of various degrees of handedness, rather than simply left- versus right-handedness.

Other dominances

We don't just have a dominant hand, however, but also a dominant eye, ear and foot. A dominant left eye and foot is thought to be responsible for the high number of successful left-handers in popular sports such as tennis and other hand–eye coordination games. Left-handers are also considered particularly advantaged in combat sports such as fencing. Interestingly, many famous left-handed sports people, such as cricketer David Gower and golfer Bob Charles are right-handers for single-handed actions such as writing and throwing, so are probably 'cross-lateral' (see below).

Cross-laterality

This is a mixture of sidedness, such as left-handed but right-footed and right-eyed. It can cause some coordination problems, and crossed hand/eye dominance can affect performance in some sports, particularly racquet sports, where the field of vision might sometimes be restricted. On the other hand, cross-laterality can be advantageous in gymnastics, running and games

---

Famous sporting left-handers

- **Tennis** Bjorn Borg, Martina Navratilova, Jimmy Connors, John McEnroe, Greg Rusedski, Goran Ivanisevic

- **Cricket** David Gower, Brian Lara

- **Baseball** Babe Ruth

- **Golf** Bob Charles, Phil Mickelson

How to determine eye dominance

To find out if your left or right eye is dominant, stretch your arm out in front of you and point at a small object some distance away, so that your finger is pointing directly at it. Now close one eye. If the finger is still directly in line with the object, then the eye you have open is your dominant eye. If you now look only with the other eye, the object will appear to shift sharply to one side of your finger. This is your non-dominant eye.

such as basketball, because positioning of the body would be more evenly distributed for better balance.

Young children may appear cross-lateral before they settle on a particular hand preference. It is important to note that cross-laterality, left-handedness and undetermined handedness are not causes of learning difficulties or disabilities (e.g. dyslexia, dyscalculia, ADD/ADHD), as we are sometimes led to believe. However, they may appear in addition to them. It is important to understand that if your child is having learning difficulties, it is unlikely to be because he is left-handed or cross-lateral, so always look further for an underlying cause.

Motor skills

For many mixed-handers, which hand or arm they choose for a particular action depends on whether it is a fine or gross motor skill (muscle movement). Gross motor skills are larger movements involving the arm, leg or feet muscles, and fine motor skills are smaller actions like picking up objects. If the muscles on the right side are stronger, this side would be used for gross motor skills such as playing racquet sports, whilst the left hand, which has more control and dexterity, is used for fine motor skills like writing.

Left-handed or left-footed players have an advantage in a number of sports.

Interconnectivity

The two hemispheres of the brain are linked by the nerves of the *Corpus callosum* (see page 18), which send messages between the two halves. As this nerve 'superhighway' can vary in size from person to person, researchers feel that it may have a direct impact on how efficiently the tasks your brain is performing on both sides can interact and complement each other.

The 'Stroop Task'

The 'Stroop Task' is a psychological test. In it, the names of colours are written in a colour of ink that is different from the colour that the words represent, for example, the word 'red' written in green followed by the word 'blue' written in yellow. To do the task, you need to name the colouring of the word instead of the colour that the word represents.

Some researchers have adopted this task to show the strength of interaction between the two halves of the brain. In this task you have to stop one of your brain's responses in order to allow it to make another response.

Reading is generally considered to be a left-hemisphere function, whereas colour recognition is a right-hemisphere task. Some research suggests that people of very mixed-handedness score lowest on such tasks, since the two sides of their brain interact more readily, and the automatic reading action interferes with the efforts to identify the colour.

This 'graduation' in handedness is also seen as highly significant when studying the location

Swapping the position of left- and right-handers at the table avoids the bumping of elbows.

A left-footer will balance on this leg and offer the right foot first for dressing.

of the speech centre in the brain. While most people have their centre of speech located in the left hemisphere, it appears that among 30 per cent of left-handers, the speech centre is spread across both hemispheres. This would seem to give them an enormous advantage in verbalizing their thought processes, creative ideas and emotions.

Degrees of difficulty

When dealing with left-handed children, it is important to realize and understand that there are varying degrees of hand dominance, so you must never assume that all left-handers will have difficulties with the same tasks. One of the most common mistakes left-handed adults make is to dismiss the difficulties of left-handed children in their care as unimportant – 'I'm left-handed, and I never had any trouble.' While many parents are reassured to know their child's teacher is also left-handed, this can sometimes bring its own problems. For example, if the teacher is mixed-handed, they may write left-handed yet be perfectly comfortable using their right hand to cut, and therefore dismiss left-handed scissors as unnecessary.

How left-handed are you?

We all know which hand we use to hold a pen, but just how far does this bias extend throughout our body? Are you right-eared? Left-footed? Mixed-handed or totally right-biased? Try these simple tests on all the family to find out:

Starter for 10

1 Imagine the centre of your back is itching. Which hand do you scratch it with?
2 Interlock your fingers. Which thumb is uppermost?
3 Imagine you are applauding. Start clapping your hands. Which hand is uppermost?
4 Wink at an imaginary friend straight in front of you. Which eye does the winking?
5 Put your hands behind your back, one holding the other. Which hand does the holding?
6 Someone in front of you is shouting, but you cannot hear the words. Cup your ear with your hand, to hear better. Which ear do you cup?
7 Count to three on your fingers using the forefinger of the other hand. Which forefinger do you use?
8 Imagine answering the phone. To which ear do you hold the receiver to listen?
9 Do the eye-dominance test on page 25. Which is your dominant eye?
10 An imaginary football is rolling towards you. Which foot would you kick it with, to get it a long way down the football field?

Through doing these simple tests you have probably discovered that your body is not totally committed to one side even if you have always considered yourself to be right- or left-handed. Very few people will do all ten tasks with one side of the body.

Gestalt – the whole picture

Your brain is always trying to make sense of your surroundings, by looking for patterns and completing pictures, often combining previously learned information with that which is in front of you. This completing of the picture is known as 'Gestalt' and is considered to be a right hemisphere function, so tasks like the one below are exercising your left-handed brain power!

The non-existent triangle test

Here's another example showing how your left-handed brain (the right hemisphere) can even create things that don't exist. If you can see the white triangle – the one with its apex pointing up – it's because your left-handed brain has created that triangle to unify what is otherwise simply a collection of angles and PacMan shapes. There is, in fact, no white triangle there.

Thurston's hand test

The left-handed brain's (right hemisphere's) mastery of the visual has an important benefit – it can 'see' three dimensionally. In Thurston's hand test, you are asked to identify which pictures are of left hands and which are of right hands. The left hemisphere of your brain is at a loss to handle this problem, but the right hemisphere can actually rotate these drawings in imaginary space to solve the test, so most left-handers will find the test easier than right-handers. Have a go!

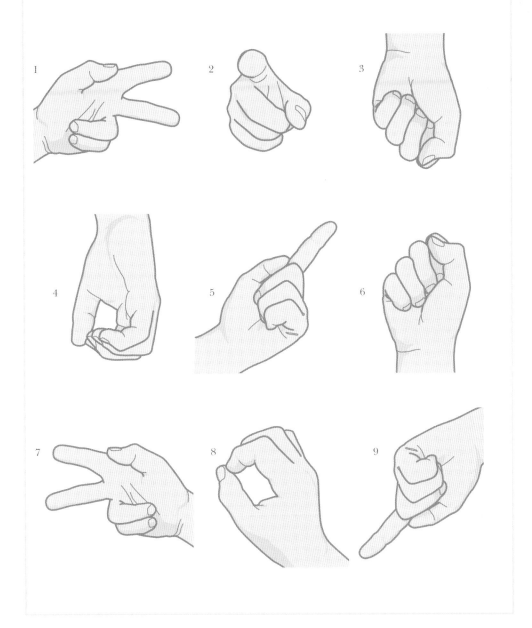

Pre-school Development

Babies and toddlers

One of the many important discoveries babies make, from the time they begin exploring the world around them, is whether they are more comfortable using their left or right hand. Through their actions they will be comparing how things feel and behave in their hands, and so which hand works best for certain tasks.

Provide toys and activities that encourage your child to develop coordination.

Early frustrations

Some babies have a strong hand preference almost from birth, but many do not show any early preference and there may be a very fluid interchange between right and left, which is quite normal since hand–eye coordination and fine motor skills are still developing (see pages 24–25). No doubt you will be following progress with interest, and if you have other children, comparing things like which thumb she prefers to suck, which hand she uses to feed herself with or uses to pick up crayons.

Having a left-handed child myself, I know that discovering the world around them can be exciting and fun, but frustrating if things don't work properly. During the early years, your child will enjoy and repeat games and tasks that give an instant reward, and quickly lose interest in those that cause frustration or do not seem to work well. By using the simple tips in this chapter, you can remove unnecessary obstacles from your child's first experiences, allowing her to explore her world with confidence and develop her skills successfully.

Because children's hand preference is sometimes slow to develop, encourage your baby or toddler to experiment with using both hands for feeding, holding and placing objects. If your child shows any preference for her left hand, you should ensure she has items that work well if used left-handed, making the task a rewarding and positive experience she will want to repeat.

Is being left-handed a problem?

Being left- or right-handed makes no difference to your child's intelligence or ability, so you need not be concerned, but it *is* important to be aware of

Some babies are strongly left-handed from birth, and some even suck their left thumb in the womb.

it, so that you can adapt your teaching and guidance techniques accordingly.

The only possible difficulties your left-handed child may encounter will be in trying to use equipment that is very biased in design to right-handed use, or through being made to work in a position that is comfortable for right-handers, yet awkward for a left-hander.

Many children struggle needlessly with the wrong equipment, layout and positioning simply because their parent or teacher has either not noticed the child was left-handed or did not know what difficulties a left-hander might encounter. Many of the examples you will find in this book will never have occurred to you. Some are little more than a nuisance, others can be potentially dangerous, yet all are obstacles that your left-handed child will encounter on a regular basis. Many can easily be avoided if your child is taught the best left-handed techniques for adapting, and has left-handed tools available where appropriate.

It's genetic

Research indicates that children's hand preference is determined by genetic make-up (see page 20), and as the brain develops, so does hand–eye coordination and fine motor skills, and they will be able to undertake increasingly intricate tasks. Handedness is *not* a matter of choice, and it is important to allow children to use the hand they prefer for various actions – even if this hand changes from day to day, as different skills develop.

Is my child left-handed?

Although some babies show they are left-handed from day one (many even suck their left thumb!), it is not uncommon for children of nursery age to still be undecided as to their dominant hand, as children develop at different rates.

Individual differences

Most babies use both hands to begin with, and rarely show any preference before about seven to nine months old. By about 18 months many children use one hand consistently. However, it is not unusual for children to show no distinct preference even at three or four years old.

Generally speaking, the earlier a child shows a specific dominance for a hand, the more strongly dominant that hand will be. It may be that if a child has no strong preference until later, even when increasing the number of manually dexterous tasks she performs as her brain and coordination develop, it is because she is comfortable using both hands. Most children have a preferred writing hand by five years old, but their brains and coordination are still developing and hand preference, too, can continue to develop until nine years old.

Early indicators

Even for children who have not decided on hand preference by the time they start nursery, you can watch their development by noting:

- Which hand they use to reach for toys and crayons placed directly in front of them.
- Which hand they prefer to feed themselves with (either finger food or spoon).
- Which hand they prefer to stir with, for example, if helping you bake a cake. Left-handers usually stir anticlockwise.
- How they draw. When drawing, or attempting to form letters, left-handers usually prefer to work from right to left, away from the body, which is a more natural movement.
- How they handle toys and implements. Left-handed children will try to turn things anticlockwise, against the thread of a screw, or to wind up a toy by unwinding it!
- Which leg they lift to hop or stand on one leg. Left-handers may feel more secure standing on the left.
- Which hand they brush their teeth or comb their hair with.

Early hand preference can suggest left-handedness.

Wind-up toys can be frustrating for left-handers, who naturally turn anticlockwise.

It is interesting to note that watching your child catch and throw a ball is not always an accurate measure of her ultimate hand preference. This is because the task involves a mixture of dominant hand and dominant eye (see Cross-laterality, page 24).

Whatever hand preference your child shows, it is important to let her develop naturally, as she will only choose the hand that is better able to complete whatever task is set, at her brain's current stage of development. Forcing her to use a particular hand early on can be damaging.

Did you know?

'Dexterous', meaning adept, efficient and skilful, is derived from the Latin word *dexter* meaning right (dextral is another word for right-handed). Thus ambidextrous literally means 'having two right hands'. The Latin for 'left' is *sinistra*, from which we derive the term 'sinister' – one of the earliest examples of right-hand prejudice!

Changing handedness?

Should you try to change your child's handedness? Emphatically 'No!'. Handedness is determined by the brain, not the hand, and the most versatile hand is that which helps the brain and hand work together for both language and writing.

Misguided thinking

Left-handed children who are made to perform a task right-handed when this is not their natural choice are using the weaker and less coordinated hand, which makes them unnecessarily clumsy, ineffective and tire more easily. Forcing children to use their less able hand is not only cruel but puts them at an enormous disadvantage. Far more practice and concentration will be needed than if using their natural hand, so the task will be less enjoyable or rewarding, making them feel less capable than they actually are.

Never change your child's handedness – help her to work more efficiently with her natural hand.

Sadly, some misguided adults still consider changing a child's handedness, usually for one of the following reasons:

- A mechanical adherence to tradition or custom
- Religious/ideological dictate
- Laziness
- Ignorance
- Social/family prejudice
- A mistaken belief it would be more practical for the child.

Adverse effects

Converting a child's hand dominance does not convert brain dominance, so you will be overloading the non-dominant side of the brain with tasks it is not intended to perform. Dr Johanna Barbara Sattler is a psychotherapist and child psychologist who has worked extensively with 'converted' left-handers in schools found throughout Germany and published many books on the subject (see Resources, pages 122–123). In her experience, Dr Sattler has found that, because of the variety of cerebral skills involved in the complex process of writing, such as fine motor skills, speech, pictorial representation of imagination, graphic representations, memory and recall of learned material, the consequences

of converting a child's handedness in writing can lead to tremendous developmental disturbances. The possible consequences include:

- Memory disorders (especially in the recall of learned material)
- Disturbances in concentration (being easily tired)
- Dyslexia (i.e. problems in reading and writing)
- Spatial disorientation (uncertainty concerning the left and right)
- Disorders in fine motor skills that manifest themselves in handwriting
- Disturbances in speech (such as stammering and stuttering).

The damage to the child's self-esteem and confidence are also incalculable, and can manifest themselves in a number of ways, including:

- Inferiority complexes
- Insecurity
- Introversion
- Over-compensation through heightened performance
- Contrariness – an oppositional and provocative manner (e.g. the class clown in school; and the persistent, compulsive wise-cracker in adulthood)
- Bedwetting and nail-biting
- Emotional problems lasting into adulthood with neurotic and/or psychosomatic symptomology
- Disorders in the personality profile.

Be positive

Even if you 'train' left-handers to perform one task right-handed, they will still always be naturally left-handed for everything else – left-handedness is part of a person's make-up, not a trend or habit that can be quashed or discouraged. With consideration and gentle encouragement, left-handers can learn to overcome many of the obstacles encountered through living in a right-handed world. They will have the confidence to explore the sporting, musical and artistic activities at which they so often excel, and in doing so become far more adaptable, confident and capable.

Goodbye to all that

Thankfully, very few teachers today reprimand their students for using the 'wrong' hand as did their Victorian counterparts, although it is still entirely possible that you may encounter adults who had been forced to write with their right hand, as this practice still continued into the last generation. However, most people now realize how unnecessarily cruel and damaging this ridiculous practice can be to a young child, based as it is on superstition, ignorance and prejudice.

Helping toddlers with daily tasks

You can help a left-handed child with everyday tasks with just a little consideration. Simply being alert to some of the different ways a left-hander approaches daily activities such as dressing and eating can enable you to help, rather than hinder, her learning.

Eating

Many people assume that they will need to reverse the cutlery for a left-hander at the dinner table, but this is often not necessary. According to studies by the Left-Handers' Association, it is very rare that left-handers reverse their cutlery, as most usually feed themselves with the left hand consistently, using the fork in the left. They do, however, usually swap the dessert or soup spoon into the left hand. An interesting point: strongly dominant right-handers often have to learn to swap over their 'fork' hand, as they prefer to use a fork in their right hand to feed as children, until social pressure takes hold when they start to use a knife and fork together.

Once they progress to adult cutlery, some left-handers do prefer to change the knife and fork round if they have trouble controlling the knife in the right hand. Correctly serrated table knives are available to accommodate them.

One trait you do need to be aware of, however, is that left-handers will frequently pick up the drink of the person to their left at the table, or eat the bread roll on their neighbour's side plate! Elbow clashes are also quite common if a right-hander is sitting to the left side of a left-hander when drinking soup with a spoon or eating food with chopsticks.

In the kitchen

As you guide your little left-hander in first attempts at mixing and pouring, it will help to place items near her left side to avoid spillages. Also remember that your left-hander will probably stir in an anticlockwise direction, holding the spoon in her left hand, so you need to do the same if you stand behind and help.

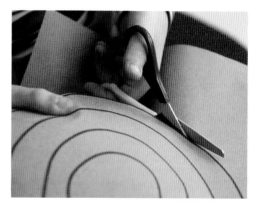
Cut clockwise with proper left-handed scissors.

Cutting out

If (as most left-handers do) your child does show a preference for using her left hand once she starts cutting out, make sure that she has a pair of proper left-handed scissors – but please remember: there is no such thing as 'universal' scissors that work in either hand. Pay particular attention to the direction she cuts out a shape. To get the best positioning and uninterrupted view of the cutting line, a left-hander should begin cutting out a shape at its left-hand bottom edge, and progress up the left side and around in a clockwise direction. Rotate the shape, not the scissors. If she has been using right-handed or so-called ambidextrous scissors, however, your child may have started cutting out anticlockwise, while bending the paper, in an effort to try and see over the blade, which will be covering up the cutting line. Explain that with her own, left-handed scissors, she doesn't need to do this. For full details on scissors and using them correctly, see page 60.

Getting dressed

- When putting on trousers, shoes or socks, you will find that left-handers usually lift their right foot first (so they can balance on the left). When helping them to dress, have the right sock or shoe or trouser leg ready first.

- Look out for pockets on both sides of clothing: if a skirt or trousers only has one pocket, it is more likely to be on the right.

- Tying knots and bows can be tricky if your little left-hander is always trying to copy your own right-handed tying methods. If you stand opposite her to show her how to tie shoelaces or ties, then your right-handed actions are automatically reversed for her to follow, like a mirror image. (See page 72 for a step-by-step guide to tying shoelaces left-handed.)

- Boys' shirts and jackets are buttoned left over right, but girls' clothes are the reverse, which usually makes them easier for left-handers to master. This tradition stems from the era when ladies were dressed by a lady's maid (assumed to be right-handed), so fastenings needed to be convenient for the dresser not the wearer.

- Traditionally, zips on trousers have followed this same convention, but some girls' trousers now have 'right-handed' zips, the same as boys', so left-handed girls may not always have it easier.

Anticipate which foot your child uses to dress.

Pre-writing skills

Children begin to understand that writing carries meaning, and to use writing in play at around four years old. Before that time, they still enjoy the immediate reward of drawing brightly coloured shapes on paper, and any attempts to wield a paintbrush or crayon should be encouraged.

Finger patterns

Finger painting is a great way for children to experiment with how their hands create shapes, the results of different pressure and movement on the paint and how to control their hand's movement across the paper. Lay down plenty of newspaper to catch any mess and let your child loose on the kitchen table!

Toddlers will want to try out all fingers and both hands to start with, but will progress to dipping a forefinger into the paint and using that finger to create a masterpiece. Encourage drawing of large circles, spirals and wavy lines (all exercises in manual control and a good pre-skill for writing), but don't attempt to influence which hand they use – it is also quite normal for them to use both at this stage. Encourage them to talk about what they are drawing, to stimulate the connection between language and the hand.

A sand box provides another fun way to practise drawing pictures and patterns. Drawing in sand using the pointed index finger, with the rest of the fingers settled into a relaxed fist, is an ideal precursor to first writing, because with the correct grip on a pencil, the index finger should still be the one dictating the movement on the paper, while the other digits just provide grip and support. Also, gently encourage keeping the hand underneath the drawing finger or paintbrush rather than beside or above it.

The tri-grip

Choose chunky crayons and oversized pencils, colouring pens and brushes, as thin, delicate barrels are harder for all little hands to control.

Lots of manufacturers now make what are called tri-grip pencils, which have three edges rather than hexagonal or round barrels, and these are great for left-handers. Their shape encourages a good left-handed 'tripod' grip, between the thumb and forefinger, with the third side resting on the middle finger for support and control. Although not important at this early age, this positioning will be hugely beneficial when your child starts forming letters. Left-handers have to push their pencil across the page, and any other grip will leave their hand covering and smudging the words. Developing the ideal writing style is covered in detail in Chapter 3 (see pages 54–59).

This positioning will take time to develop, as left-handers often grip their drawing tools in a fist or use all fingers to start with, but if you are aware that this is your ultimate goal, you can gradually encourage this positioning as your child's finger control develops. Lead by example, using your own left hand to write and draw (however strange the results!) and encourage your child to copy your pencil grip. Correct only gently, with lots of praise, otherwise you risk putting your child off writing from an early age.

Keep their options open

Always place crayons, toys and implements in front of young children so they can reach easily with either hand, and don't worry if they change hands frequently when first trying out drawing.

Let your child experiment with her hands using paint, paintbrushes and colouring pens.

The ideal position: a three-finger grip with the hand underneath the brush.

Fluidity of movement

Wherever possible, give your child the opportunity to draw in a large, relaxed space with big paper, either on the floor or, ideally, standing at an easel or whiteboard. Keep the easel high so your child is drawing slightly above her shoulder height and stand her to the right of the easel or whiteboard, so her arm is to the left of her body and she has plenty of room to bring it towards her across the page. Encourage big, sweeping movements of the brush or crayon. Patterns with continuous circles and spirals that will later lead on to letter formation are good, as are rhythmic up/down and back/forth lines zig-zagging across the page. Put on some music and get your child to draw to the rhythm. Rhythmic movement is very important for fluency, so the patterns should be drawn quickly. Progress to big waves, fluffy clouds, train tracks or any patterns or shapes that have elements of letters in them.

Direction of shapes and patterns

You may notice that your left-hander often draws or paints circles anticlockwise and horizontal lines from right to left, bringing the brush or pencil back towards the left-hand side of her body. This direction gives less drag on the brush or pen, so it works more smoothly. This is absolutely fine for single shapes and small lines, as these directional strokes can be incorporated into cursive writing without any difficulty later on. However, once your child progresses to making patterns, or pretend writing, you can explain that real words start at the left of the page and work towards the right. This is an unnatural direction for left-handers, and needs to become a learned habit over time.

It is quite common for left-handers to start at the right of the page and progress towards the left, often forming perfect mirror images of letters that they can read perfectly well. A small sticker or drawing a star in the top left of a blank page is helpful to remind them where to start. You can casually reinforce this directionality in a number of ways – try pointing out interesting signs and notices, playing word-building games, and encourage your child to follow the lines you read in storybooks with her finger.

First writing

Although it is not necessary or advisable to do too much work with children before they start school, being gently guided by a relaxed and enthusiastic parent in the fundamental basics for good writing will be a huge help in later life, provided the emphasis is on the rhythm of writing, and the fun of creating pretty patterns and shapes. The fundamental points you can work into drawing games at home are:

- Not holding a pencil or crayon too tightly

- Grasping it between thumb and forefinger rather than in a fist

- Having the paper slightly to the left side of the body and slanted towards the right

- Scribbles and patterns run in a left-to-right direction.

It is far more important to focus on pre-reading skills than to try to teach reading or writing to a child who is not ready, so only approach this topic when your child seems willing and interested to learn. Never make writing a chore, only practise for a few minutes at first and at the first sign of stress or tiredness, swap to another activity.

Toys and games

Your child's preference for using one hand over the other for certain tasks also extends to the rest of the body. The effects of a dominant left hand counterbalanced by a dominant right foot or eye shows up particularly in sports.

Advantages and disadvantages of cross-laterality

Everyone has a dominant eye, ear and foot as well as hand – although which side is not necessarily consistent. As explained on page 24, this is called cross-laterality. Not surprisingly, a mixture of sidedness (such as left-handed but right-footed and right-eyed) has advantages and disadvantages. Cross-laterality can sometimes cause coordination problems in children, but also give them an edge in some sports.

Young children may appear cross-lateral before they settle on a particular hand preference. Crossed hand/eye dominance can affect your child's performance in some sports, particularly racquet sports where the field of vision might sometimes be restricted. This may make your child appear clumsy, but try to appreciate that in fact he has to work a lot harder to achieve accuracy and deserves all your patience and encouragement to persevere.

Development varies from child to child, but don't be surprised to see your left-hander using his right foot to kick a ball, or even use his right hand to catch, despite seeming very left-handed otherwise. This disparity is often due to the dominant eye as much as the hand or foot, as catching a ball, or aiming accurately rely a great deal on hand–eye coordination. This explains why some excellent left-handed cricketers and

Your child also has a dominant foot, ear and eye.

Out of left field

Your little leftie may develop a secret advantage when playing with frisbee flying discs. If commonly playing with right-handers, he will learn to catch throws that spin clockwise, but often a right-hander has difficulty catching a frisbee thrown by a left-hander because it is spinning the opposite way, and he is not used to it!

baseball players are actually right-handed writers – they may have a dominant right eye and find it easier to catch/throw with their left hand because of it.

Champion lefties

Children who show an aptitude for playing sport left-handed are in good company! Left-handers are said to have an advantage in sports that demand rapid reactions and good spatial judgement. Judging distances is a 'left-handed brain' function, and a vital skill in sports like fencing (where reaction times are short, and the proportion of left-handed champions extremely high) and tennis (where left-handers Navratilova, Connors, McEnroe, Ivanisevic, Seles, Lendl, Rusedski and many more have triumphed).

Many left-handers become adept at changing hands for different tasks, and some left-handed tennis players can switch the racquet from one hand to the other with ease. In baseball and cricket, many left-handers bat right-handed and bowl with the left.

Another contributory factor in left-handers' sporting success is their regular training against right-handed opponents, while right-handers are often not used to playing against a left-hander.

Learning through play

As parents, we need to appreciate the importance of developing all areas of our children's ability, not just their natural strengths. Pages 46–47 feature some examples of classic activities and educational games that immediately appeal to the common strengths left-handed children exhibit, such as creativity, imagination, spatial judgement and good mental 3-D imagery, while reinforcing the hand–eye coordination, manipulative skills and reading/writing directionality that are often slower to develop. While he is busy having fun, your child will also be strengthening the logical, mathematical and language skills so fundamental to basic learning, and encouraging interaction between the two sides of the brain to help him develop to the best of his potential.

Provide toys and games that encourage hand–eye coordination.

Toys with handles should work in either direction.

Mosaic and peg boards

These are a great way to experiment with colours and develop hand–eye coordination and manual skills. The brightly coloured pegs stimulate the strategic-thinking and problem-solving skills as your child tries to compose pictures.

Playing cards and card games

Traditionally, playing cards only have the number on two opposite corners, which cannot be seen when fanned in the left hand. Check that playing cards have the numbers printed in all four corners before you buy them.

Sewing cards and threading toys

Threading the coloured wool through fun pictures, or creative craft kits suitable for inexperienced little hands help improve dexterity and manipulative skills. Allied to these are lacing cards to help young children learn to tie their shoelaces (see page 72).

Moving toys

Traditional wind-up toys need winding in a clockwise direction, and can be frustrating for left-handers, who naturally turn anticlockwise. (If your toddler seems to be holding the 'key' still with the right hand and winding the toy itself round and round, it may be a sign that they are left-handed!) Also, the handle or control is often on the right side of the object, so a left-hander has to hold it upside down to make it work. Even if she can reach the winding key comfortably with the left hand, she may then wind the wrong way – be aware of this if your child seems annoyed or frustrated with the toy, or the key keeps screwing off.

Look for levers, knobs and handles that work when turned either way, and are located within easy reach of the left hand. Interlocking gears work well, and produce an instant reward when turned in either direction. Construction toys (suited to your child's age) with plenty of gears, plates and characters to put together are excellent for hand–eye coordination and fine motor skill development, and demonstrate basic mechanics.

Threading beads helps coordination skills.

Word games

First sequence games using pictures that join up from left to right to make a story are an excellent way to encourage the right-to-left direction ready for reading and writing. What comes after a seed? What happens after you fall asleep? Joining the puzzle pieces in the correct direction gives the answer. You can progress to games that include letter shapes with the pictures. Again, these are great for reinforcing word direction and letter shapes, and the pictures mean pre-readers can play as well.

Cutting out shapes

Once your child has left-handed safety scissors, cutting activities will help her develop scissor control without even noticing! Cutting circles and spirals gives excellent practice and a selection of cutting skills can also be downloaded from www.lefthandedchildren.org. (See also page 60 for information on choosing and using scissors.)

Computers

Children are encouraged to use computers from a very early age nowadays, and there are lots of computer games for pre-school children available.

Using a computer mouse requires a very precise skill. Not all left-handers need to use a mouse in their left hand, but they do need the opportunity to compare which hand is better at controlling it. Otherwise, they will simply be slow and laboured in using it right-handed, or develop lifelong bad postural habits. For really easy mouse-swapping, see page 68. A trackball is a good alternative to a conventional mouse. It looks like an upside down mouse, with the tracker ball on top, which rolls very easily using the palm or fingers of either hand.

Some computer joysticks can also be adapted so that the control buttons are situated under the left thumb and fingers – important if your little left-hander is to have a fighting chance against his right-handed opponent!

Arts and crafts can be hugely rewarding – provided you have the proper scissors!

Top tips for pre-schoolers

At this early age, many children are probably not aware of the concept of 'left and right', and it is quite likely that some of them have not yet settled on their eventual hand preference. If you feel your child may be left-handed, but are not sure, ask her new teacher simply to be patient, encouraging and supportive. Pass on the following tips as appropriate to the new nursery or pre-school.

Daily tasks

Eating Left-handers tend to feed themselves with their left hand all the time (dinner fork and pudding spoon) – they don't often reverse the cutlery, unless they are trying to cut with a knife, when they will be better using this in their left hand.

Dressing For left-handed boys, buttons and zips are 'back to front' so need a bit more practice. When helping left-handers with trousers/shoes, remember they usually balance on their left foot first, so have the right leg/shoe ready for them to step in to.

Shoelaces/ties A good tip is to stand *opposite* the child when demonstrating tying a tie or laces. This provides them with a mirror image to copy.

Baking/stirring Left-handers will want to use the spoon in their left hand and stir anticlockwise, so do the same if you are helping them. Put ingredients to the left of the bowl so they can pour them in easily.

Wind-up toys If a left-hander is frustrated with a toy, it may be because it works back-to-front for her. See recommended alternatives in resources section on pages 122–123.

Cutting Do ensure your child has access to fully left-handed scissors for all craft work. Find out how left-handed scissors are distinguished (for instance with different coloured handles or ribbons) and ensure your child understands the difference, and knows to ask for her type of scissors. Check that there are enough pairs for all the left-handers in the group to use, and they are not given out to right-handers by mistake!

Computers If the nursery or pre-school offers computers to play on, check out page 68 for tips on left-handers and mice.

Drawing and writing

Make sure you know all the necessary tips for training left-handers to write before starting to show them this skill (see page 55 and you can also visit www.lefthandedchildren.org for writing resources).

Direction Many pre-school children are still experimenting with both hands for writing, drawing and other skills, and this will continue until they develop enough to have stronger accuracy in one. You may need to remind left-handers to start at the top left side of the page.

Pencils and crayons Oversized triangular crayons and pencils help develop the ideal tripod grip that left-handers need to avoid smudging and cramped grip as they learn to write. Always ensure pencils/crayons/toys and so on are placed directly in front within easy reach of either hand.

Painting at an easel Leave enough room for a left-hander to stand slightly to the right of the easel as she works, or she will be working across her body, which makes her hook her arm round.

Check your crèche or nursery notice left-handedness and can cater to your child's needs.

Which hand?

Ambivalence over handedness is quite normal, particularly in left-handers who sometimes take longer to finally settle on their dominant hand. It is essential not to pressurize them into deciding too early, but allow them to experiment with either hand as they see fit. Remember, left-handers are exploring a world where many things work back to front, and they will need your guidance and patience to help them adapt some things to work properly for them.

' When any child joins my crèche I get them to cut out, so we all know which scissors they should use. Even the little ones who don't really understand about being left- or right-handed can remember whether they need "blue scissors" or "red scissors" for cutting! '

Jo Hopkins, childcare supervisor.

Strategies for Everyday Life

Things that are difficult

Being left-handed is not a problem – but using right-bias equipment can be!
Having to work in an awkward space or approach a task from the wrong angle will
inevitably present your child with extra difficulties not encountered by the right-
handed members of the family. Look at your home from a left-hander's viewpoint,
and see what you can do to avoid potential difficulties.

The right-handed positioning of this kettle means
the left-hander is forced to pour backwards.

Safety first

As your child gets older, he will probably start to
help you around the house and garden, and it is
vital that is given full consideration when
undertaking any new task. Accidents can happen
to anyone, in any household, but it is beyond
doubt that some of the accidents left-handers
have are caused by awkward or untrained use of
equipment that has a right-hand bias.

It would be impossible to document all the
tools and equipment your child is likely to come
across in your home, but it is important to be
aware that the more powerful the tool the more
dangerous it can be if used incorrectly.
Awareness, training and extra caution may be
enough to avert any potential accidents, so you
must spend time teaching your child how to use
tools and equipment. Most accidents occur
because tools are not being used correctly, not
because the child is 'naturally clumsy'.

Things to consider

Before you introduce an implement to your
child, look at it carefully and consider the
following points:

- Where and how it is gripped

- The direction of force needed

- Where the controls and safety cut-out
  switch (if applicable) are positioned.

Your little one will stir anticlockwise with her left hand, so remember to do the same!

Try it yourself

Put yourself in your child's place. Try holding a tool in your left hand and manipulating the controls to see if it can be operated safely by a left-hander. Many power tools such as drills and saws will have a right-handed bias. Dials, buttons and safety cut-out switches are often positioned for a right-hander's convenience and grips are ergonomically moulded to fit an adult right hand.

If you feel a tool cannot be safely held and used by a left-hander, do not allow your child to have access to it. Even if, after careful thought, you feel happy your child can use the tool, do ensure you spend as much time as necessary training her, so that you both feel confident it will be used safely, comfortably and confidently. Naturally, your child should always be supervised when using tools.

Writing

There is absolutely no reason why your left-handed child should not develop a neat, comfortable and efficient handwriting style, but it will take the correct guidance, patient teaching and lots of encouragement.

Common problems

This basic and very necessary skill can cause left-handed children real trouble for several reasons.

Pushing instead of pulling Writing from left to right means having to push a pen or pencil across the paper, rather than pulling it like a right-hander. This tends to make the point dig into the paper rather than flowing smoothly, which can interrupt the flow and rhythm necessary for a relaxed, fluid writing style.

Uncomfortable grip To gain control, left-handers are inclined to use as many fingers as possible. They hold the pen far too tightly, and press down too hard on the paper, which makes their letter formation difficult and leads to a cramped hand.

Awkward position Without specific guidance in the correct left-handed paper position and grip, they will adopt their own writing style. This often means adopting an awkward and uncomfortable posture, leading to aching wrist, back and neck.

Knocking elbows is a common problem easily resolved by swapping places or seating left-handers together.

Things that help

Many of these problems can be solved fairly easily by following these guidelines. Remember to keep emphasizing your child's achievements with lots of praise and make allowances for clumsiness, smudging and untidiness as her writing develops and gradually improves.

- For younger children, choose a soft pencil, one which does not stick or tear the paper. Older children should be encouraged to experiment with different pens and pencils to find one that flows smoothly across the page. Left-handed fountain pens have angled nibs that don't catch on the paper and encourage the ink to flow smoothly (see page 58).

- Show your child how to hold the pencil at least 2 cm (just under 1 inch) away from the tip so that her fingers do not obscure what she is writing.

- Place the paper at a slight angle in a position that encourages a good posture (see pages 56–57).

- Encourage a comfortable and efficient grip (see page 56).

- Put a star or sticker on the top left margin of a new page to remind your child to write from left to right (mirror writing is very common with left-handers who are just learning how to write).

- Use left-handed letter formations, and left-handed practice workbooks to reinforce correct grip, posture, paper position and letter formation (see page 59).

- For a school child who sits at a shared desk, talk to her teacher about sitting with another left-hander or to the left side of a right-hander (to avoid knocking elbows).

Poor ink flow These problems are made even worse when left-handed children have to start writing with a proper nib in a cartridge or fountain pen. Regular nibs are designed to slide on the paper and give a smooth ink flow when pulled with the right hand. When pushed across the paper with the *left* hand, the nib scratches and ink flow is sporadic.

Smudging When left-handers progress to using ink pens, they find that as the hand follows their work, it smudges the writing they have produced, so they start to move the hand up, up, and up further until it is curled round in the 'hooked' writing position so characteristic of many left-handers. The hand is now above the writing line with the pencil tilted in the same direction a right-hander would have, so the pen works more efficiently, but their whole body is contorted to achieve it.

An overtight grip with the hand following the words will lead to smudging and bad posture.

Good grip, good posture

Developing a good position and grip for writing right from the outset will overcome the natural difficulties in writing in 'the wrong direction' and avoid having to unlearn bad habits.

The tripod grip

The best technique for a left-hander is the three-finger or 'tripod' grip. The pencil should be held lightly between the thumb and forefinger, and rest lightly on the bent middle finger. With the hand underneath the writing line, the forefinger then guides the pencil or pen to make the letter shapes, while the other fingers just act as support. The wrist and shoulders should remain relaxed as the arm slides across the page, maintaining the straight wrist and hand position. Moulded grips can help, as can fat, triangular pencils and pens (see page 40).

A comfortable posture

To prevent writing becoming a strain, your child's shoulders should be square on to the desk or table, and relaxed. Instead of placing the paper straight in front and parallel to the edge of the writing surface, place it a little off to the left and tilted clockwise up to a maximum of 45 degrees. The top right corner should be about opposite the middle of the body.

Grip tips

- The pen barrel should rest in the 'V' of the thumb and forefinger, angled towards the left shoulder, not pointing straight up at right angles from the paper.

- To lighten a tight grip and heavy pressure, try a pencil grip for correct finger position and make a game of writing on three sheets of paper with carbon paper between them – the aim is to write lightly enough *not* to make an imprint on the underneath pages.

- To maintain the correct arm and hand position and avoid it drifting up into a 'hook' shape as your child's writing progresses across the page, he should practise sweeping the hand lightly across the page from left to right a few times, without losing position. Suggest he leans back a little, and try drawing some light lines quickly across the page, while imagining that he is sweeping pencil shavings off the page with his arm at the same time!

The ideal grip

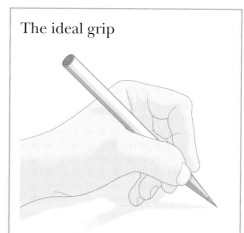

The pen is held between thumb and forefinger, resting on the middle finger. The hand is relaxed and sits below the line of writing.

The perfect writing position, with good posture, hand position, grip and paper angle.

Always make sure that your child has ample room to the left of his desk or workspace to enable him to position his work in this way. This offset position means he will be pulling the pen towards his body as he writes – a much smoother action – and have a clear view of his writing. The angle of the paper makes the start of the line too long a reach to curl the hand behind the pen, so should automatically bring the hand into the correct writing position – underneath the writing line. With the wrist straight, the hand will no longer be tempted to curve over the top of the line or follow behind the writing and smudge. The right hand should rest flat on the writing page to keep it still, well away from the writing line.

Position of the paper

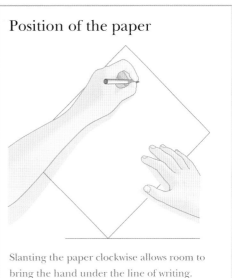

Slanting the paper clockwise allows room to bring the hand under the line of writing.

Writing implements

There are now quite a number of pens, pencils and other aids available to help left-handers acquire and maintain a good writing style. They come in a wide range of funky styles and colours designed to keep your child interested in handwriting.

Triangular barrels encourage the three-finger grip.

Triangular pencils and pens

Although not specifically for left-handers, pens, pencils and crayons that have triangular barrels help small hands develop better writing and drawing skills. The triangular shape encourages an improved grip (see page 56), which is more comfortable, provides better control and reduces writing fatigue. They are suitable for all ages, but ones with oversized barrels are easier for little hands to manoeuvre and grip.

Pencil grips

These moulded grips slide over normal-sized pencils and have specific indents for each finger, to encourage the correct writing grip.

Cartridge/fountain pens

The problems left-handers have with a traditional ink pen (difficulty with ink flow, the possibility of the nib digging into the paper) are greatly alleviated by the use of a left-handed pen. This has the nib cut off in the other direction or has a rounded ball at the end of the nib that allows it to write smoothly when being pushed. The nib design is also reversed so that the ink will flow smoothly with the left side of the nib pressed to the paper rather than the right. These differences in a small nib may not look very significant, but they make a huge difference when your child is learning to write (and for the rest of his life). A wide range of left-handed pens are available from specialists suppliers, including children's pens that feature a rubberized grip to reduce tension from an overtight grip and a ridge to prevent the fingers slipping on to the inky nib (see Resources, pages 122–123).

Calligraphy/oblique nibs

Some left-handers prefer the slight angle found on a left-handed calligraphic nib, where the tip of the nib is angled rather than being flat on. A similar effect can be produced by purchasing an oblique nib for your existing fountain pen, and a

Pencil grips train fingers in the correct writing grip.

range of left-handed calligraphy sets is available. Pen manufacturers have different names for their oblique nibs, and a left-hand oblique could slant in either direction depending on the manufacturer! It is best to try out oblique nibs in the shop before buying one to make a comparison and find the one that best suits your child's writing style.

Rollerball ink pens

A recent innovation is a rollerball pen designed for left-handers, developed after carefully studying the most comfortable and efficient position for the left-hander to write most effectively and then moulding the pen body to fit exactly that position. The pen remains perfectly placed while writing, with little or no effort, and requires the lightest of grip on the moulded rubber fingerplate.

Non-smudge fibretips

An older child, or one who experiences learning difficulties, may be unable or unwilling to adopt a writing style that prevents smudging. In this case, there are fibretip pens available that have very quick drying ink so they don't smudge, even immediately after writing. The barrel shape also provides a better grip for a 'hook'-handed style. (This awkward style is not to be encouraged, but if change is too difficult, at least the problem of smudging will be overcome, which will dispense with one discouragement.)

Offset nibs improve the view of the writing line.

Pens with offset tips

These pens, with their quirky-looking angled tip, ensure that left-handers can clearly see what they are writing as their hand does not obstruct their field of vision. A rubber tripod grip rotates to the most comfortable writing position, while the offset portion of the pen prevents fingers from slipping down towards the pen tip, allowing for a more relaxed grip and keeping the hand away from the writing line, which prevents smudging. A pencil version with an offset leadholder is also available. This unusual offset design is very effective and can alleviate many of the common writing problems left-handers face when writing.

Writing mats

There are on the market writing mats specially designed to prevent or correct smudged work, poor pen grip and bad posture. These mats show the perfect paper position, pen hold and angle of the arm to achieve the most comfortable and effective style of writing as a left-hander, and are printed with child-friendly reminders about pen grip, position and letter formation charts. The same information for right-handers is usually printed on the reverse.

Ergonomic pens fit the left-hand writing position.

Using scissors

Children who have not experienced using left-handed scissors will not realize how much easier they are to use, and in struggling with a right-handed pair are unlikely to blame the scissors. More likely, they will assume they are simply 'no good at cutting out' and may well begin to avoid tasks involving the use of scissors.

What's the problem?

When young children first start to cut out shapes with scissors it is a big step, and can be a very frustrating one if they find they can't do it and everyone else can. They won't understand why they can't follow the cutting line easily, why the paper tears or buckles more than in their classmates' hands and why their hands ache so much. Faced with these difficulties, your left-handed child's first thought is likely to be 'why can't I cut?', not 'what's wrong with the scissors?', but if they are right-handed scissors, it's the scissors that are at fault.

When cutting a circle, for example, right-handers would commence at the right of the circle and proceed up and anticlockwise to cut. The top blade is on the right-hand side so it is easy to see the cutting line as they cut.

Left-handers naturally would do the opposite – start on the left side and work up and clockwise around the shape. However, with right-handed

scissors held in the left hand, the top blade obscures the cutting line, so it cannot be seen to cut accurately. To overcome this the left-hander might try to cut the shape anticlockwise, holding the paper at a slant so they can peer over the blade. However, as the blades shut, the bottom blade cuts a blade-width away from the cutting line, so left-handers need to constantly readjust their scissors and 'guess' where to cut as they cannot use the top blade as an accurate guide to the cutting line.

On left-handed scissors the blades are set the other way, so that the left blade is on top (i.e. emerging on top of the paper as you cut). This means that the cutting action of the left hand pushes the blades together to give a smooth cut the whole length of the blades and allows a clear view of the cutting line. With properly designed left-handed scissors the natural cutting action matches that of the scissors and the child just has to hold the scissors straight and naturally and not try to twist the blades. Cutting out shapes becomes a doddle! Parents are often amazed at how good the child they thought was 'hopeless at cutting anything' has become when she first tries a pair of left-handed scissors.

Other difficulties

The action of cutting normally forces the blades of the scissors together, making a tight, sharp cut. However, when held in the opposite hand, this action is reversed and the blades are slightly forced apart. To counteract this, left-handers using right-handed scissors often adopt a squeezing motion, putting undue pressure on the grips with their thumb to try to force the blades tighter together. This is, like many left-handers'

Left-handed scissors vs right-handed scissors

In the pictures on page 62, you can see the awkward style left-handers need to develop when trying to get right-handed scissors to work adequately for them in their left hand. Even after much practice however, the result will never be as good as if using a proper pair of fully left-handed scissors for the task.

The right-handed scissors in the bottom left picture obscure the cutting line and bend the paper.

adaptations and work-arounds, not a conscious decision but a manner of holding the scissors adopted over time and experience of what makes right-handed scissors work as effectively as possible in the left hand.

This squeezing action pushes the thumb joint against the scissor handle, causing sore knuckles and eventually calluses. For this reason, left-handers sometimes find left-handed scissors strange for a few seconds when they first use them, as they are not cutting with a relaxed straightforward manner, or holding the paper straight. Once they do, they are away and running!

Scissors used in the wrong hand will also serve to weaken the scissor joint, blunt the blade and shorten the life of the scissors. This applies equally to left-handed scissors used in the right hand, though of course this rarely happens!

Can I buy truly ambidextrous scissors?

The short answer is no – but be warned! Some manufacturers and educational suppliers misleadingly call their scissors 'universal' or 'suitable for left- and right-handers'. In authentic left-handed scissors the blades are completely reversed, and there can be no version that works equally well in both hands.

What manufacturers actually mean by 'ambidextrous' or 'universal' is that the handles

---

Right- and left-handed scissors

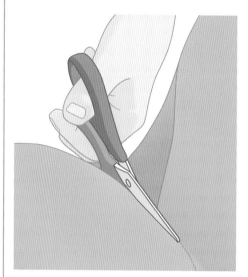

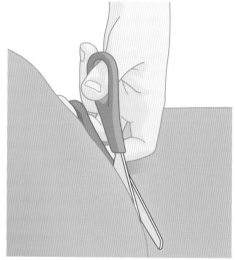

Using right-handed scissors in the left hand, the blades cover the cutting line, so children try and use them backwards to overcome this. Using scissors in the wrong hand pushes the blades apart rather than together, bending and tearing the paper rather than cutting it. Developing a strong squeezing action to overcome this problem leads to aching hands and eventually calluses.

With the blades of the scissors reversed so that the left blade is on top, left-handed children can see the cutting line and and no effort is needed to keep the blades together and get a clean accurate cut. The paper can be kept straight, and the hand relaxed. The grips of the scissor handles are also moulded to fit comfortably around a left-hander's thumb joint.

are not specifically designed for right-hand use. The design of modern plastic scissor grips is such that they are often moulded to fit the contours of the thumb knuckle to ensure a better grip and eradicate any pressure on the right thumb joint. When held in the left hand, these grips are even more uncomfortable on the left thumb joint and soon start to hurt. Scissors labelled 'suitable for right- and left-hand use' have simply reverted to the unmoulded form of handle, or moulded the thumb handle slightly to fit round both left and right thumb knuckles. They still have right-handed blades, so the main difficulties are exactly the same as a standard right-handed scissor.

Are they left-handed scissors?

You can easily check if a pair of scissors are left-handed, as whichever way up you hold them, as you cut, the left blade is always showing on top of the paper.

For stockists of left-handed scissors, and a link to a video about why left-handed scissors are important, see Resources, pages 122–123.

This right-hander is able to clearly see the cutting line, as she doesn't have to peer over the top blade.

Using right-handed scissors, this left-hander is trying to cut anticlockwise so she can see the cutting line.

Other cutting tools

Scissors are probably the first cutting implements that a child encounters, but it is helpful to be aware of difficulties that left-handers may encounter with blades of all sorts. If a left-handed version is available it can help left-handers cut more accurately and more safely.

Craft knives

The blade on a craft knife is extremely sharp, so the correct design and a comfortable secure grip in the left-hand is absolutely vital. Choose a craft knife that has a trapezoid-shaped blade with a dual edge so it can be easily set up to work for a left-hander, and the blade position changed for a right-hander if required.

Models with a safety retractable blade use the left thumb to push out the blade for use, but the pressure while cutting keeps the blade out without any further use of the thumb. Once the blade is lifted from the cutting surface, the blade automatically retracts back into the handle. An auto-locking craft knife has the same shaped blade, but can be locked into different cutting positions. A non-slip rubber grip makes these knives more comfortable and accurate to use. **Caution:** Craft knives should only be used by older children, under adult supervision.

This craft knife is for left-handed use.

Pruning shears

If your child likes to help you in the garden, it is worth noting that the same principle applies to bypass pruning shears or secateurs as it does to scissors. Left-handed versions are available in various sizes, all with the blades reversed, and not only will they be easier for your child to use, they will save your plants from the stress and danger of infection that can result from a jagged cut. Alternatively, use anvil pruning shears, which do not work on the 'scissor' principle but have a single blade hitting a flat cutting surface, and can be used in either hand.

Dinner knives

The majority of left-handers eat in the usual way, with the fork in the left hand and knife in the right, so a left-handed dinner knife would not be necessary. However, some left-handers prefer to swap their knife and fork into the other hands, in which case a properly serrated left-handed dinner knife is worth having, as it gives an easier, cleaner and more accurate cut.

Kitchen knives

Irrespective of which way they hold their cutlery for eating, nearly all left-handers will hold a knife in the left hand when using it for cutting bread, slicing food, peeling vegetables or carving meat. Once your child is old enough and ready to use knives in the kitchen, it is worth investing in some left-handed knives. Wrongly serrated knives tend to slip away from the cutting line, so your child would be much safer and more accurate if given a proper left-handed version to use (see box opposite).

Advantages of left-handed knives

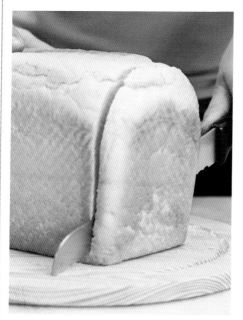

The serrations are on the right side of the blade to counterbalance the natural inward twisting motion of the left hand, giving a nice straight cut and an evenly sliced loaf.

The serrations on a normal bread knife exaggerate the natural twisting motion of the left hand leading to a curved slice and an overhanging loaf.

Serrations

In Japan, sushi knives are very specifically angled on the right side for left-hand cutting and on the left side for right-hand cutting. Elsewhere in the world confusion arises because some manufacturers make their 'normal' knives serrated on the right of the blade – the 'left-hander' side. There seems to be no definitive guidelines for which side to serrate, and most manufacturers have never really considered it, but left-handers can certainly tell the difference in the accuracy of the cut, the neatness of the slices and the increased control over the blade.

Most 'normal' knives for right-handers are serrated on the *left* of the blade – the idea being that the effect of the serrations counteracts the natural inward (clockwise as you see it) twisting action of the right hand, leading to a straight cut. If a left-hander uses one of these knives, the serrations actually emphasize the natural anticlockwise twisting motion of the left hand, which leads to the classic 'overhanging' slice. Look for knives that are serrated on the *right* side of the blade to give the correct balanced action for left-handers.

In the kitchen

The kitchen is a prime example of right-hand bias, full of gadgets that left-handers have to use in an awkward, clumsy fashion, which results in spills, scraped knuckles and patronizing glances from the rest of the family.

Taps, bottles and jars

When turning things, pushing the hand outwards and away from the body is a motion that gives far more power and control than turning inwards, towards the body. To a left-hander this means an anticlockwise movement. So when going to open bottles and jars, turn taps or handles, a left-hander's natural tendency is to turn in the 'wrong' direction to that in which they are designed to work – bear this in mind if you find your child turning a water tap further on rather than off, and valiantly trying to screw a bottle top back on without any effect. When he grows up, the same problem will occur with corkscrews!

Can openers

Positioning is awkward when using a right-handed can opener, as it has to be placed on the right side of the can, and the weaker right hand used to turn the rotary handle. The right thumb soon tires of pushing, long before the can is fully open, so often left-handers swap grip, so they are holding the handles together with the right hand, but crossing their arm over their body to reach the rotary handle and turn it with their left thumb. Although they are now using their stronger hand, the contorted position is not only awkward, but with the sharp edge of the can close by, very dangerous if the can slips, as it is prone to do.

Good and bad technique

A left-hander is forced to adopt an awkward technique when using a right-handed opener.

This left-handed opener sits on the left of the can and so the butterfly is easily pushed round.

This peeler has a left-handed blade and left-angled handle so can be pulled smoothly towards the body.

A much better option is to invest in a left-handed can opener, which provides more comfort and control. It is held in the right hand and the cutting wheel attached to the left side of the can. The rotary handle can then be turned away from you with the left hand, on the left side of the can – allowing left-handers to use their stronger and more comfortable hand.

Openers are also available that sit on the top of the can, with a handle that can be turned either way, and work equally well for left- and right-handers. A word of warning though – they do slice the entire top off the can, leaving an extremely sharp edge, which can be very dangerous, so they are not recommended for children to use unless supervised by an adult.

Peeling fruit and vegetables

The best motion for peeling fruit and vegetables is to pull the peeler towards the body, keeping the left thumb resting on the fruit and drawing the peeler towards it, in a relaxed controlled action. This is not possible with a right-handed peeler held in the left hand as the cutting edge is facing the wrong way. For this reason, many left-handers have developed a technique for peeling vegetables by moving the peeler away from the body, in a kind of whittling action that sends peelings splattering all over the sink. Unfortunately, this provides little control over the peeler, often resulting in scraped knuckles. Ensure your peeler is either fully left-handed or double-edged, for use in either direction.

Electronic equipment

Electronic equipment is not without its challenges. Some advances in electronics and software are making equipment easier for left-handers to use, while others are increasing the difficulties.

Mouse control may be easier with the left hand.

Computers

Not all left-handers find they need to use a mouse in their left hand, but they should be able to experiment, to see which hand gives the better control and is more comfortable. If they are not at ease manipulating a mouse right-handed, they will find using a computer – increasingly a part of everyone's lives – awkward and slow, or develop the bad habit of crossing their left hand over the body to reach the mouse, leading to bad posture and much backache in years to come!

If your child does prefer to use a mouse left-handed, your standard mouse buttons can be easily reconfigured through the computer's operating system (see box).

An ergonomic mouse may be too right-handed in design to be comfortable in the left. There are models of left-handed ergonomic mice available (see Resources, pages 122–123), but a standard, unmoulded mouse would be fine for general use.

Mouse swap

Check your manual or on-screen help system for 'mouse settings'. One of the options will be to switch the primary and secondary buttons and this usually involves just ticking a box to make the right mouse button the primary click. This is perfect if you are using the mouse left-handed.

As most computers are shared by right and left-handed users, it is inconvenient to keep switching back and forth in the settings and

you can solve this by obtaining some simple free software that automates the process and allows you to switch between left- and right-handed operation with a single keystroke (for instance, by pressing the F12 key).

Some models of computer use a mouse with a single button that works equally well to the left or right of the keyboard without the need to change any settings.

Another common discomfort associated with computers is the number pad, which is traditionally placed to the right of the main keyboard, making it uncomfortable for left-handers to use and often causing RSI (repetitive strain injury) if a left-hander has to do a lot of data entry. Left-handed keyboards are now available with the number pad on the left side of the qwerty keyboard, or it might be a useful skill for your child to invest a little time in learning to touch-type, and use the number keys at the top of the keyboard. There are many free touch-typing tutorial programmes on the internet.

Video games

Video games with hand-held controllers generally encourage flexibility in both hands, with each hand controlling different functions at the same time. While some controllers and joysticks have the facility to reconfigure the buttons to assign different functions, this is unlikely to offer much benefit if both hands are used.

When using the stylus in some interactive consoles, the screen can be flipped if necessary by choosing the handedness option within the game settings so it is more comfortable for left-hand use.

Some research suggests that the ability to perform and react to several tasks and stimuli at the same time is greater in left-handers, giving them an advantage not only in many sports, but also in playing video games!

Cameras and video cameras

One of the most common requests left-handers make of specialist suppliers is for camera and video equipment with controls that have easier access for the left hand. Point and shoot cameras are rarely a problem, unless the right hand is particularly weak, and the common annoyance of trying to line up the shot in a right-eye positioned viewfinder using a dominant left eye has largely been overcome in digital cameras with the use of the preview screen.

More specialized cameras and video cameras, however, are becoming increasingly ergonomic, and, as is usually the case, the term 'ergonomic' actually means 'right-hand friendly'.

Unfortunately, despite regular requests of manufacturers, there seems little likelihood of left-handed versions being produced. The huge variety of styles, makes, features and prices, plus the constant advances in technology make it impossible to create a single left-handed video camera that would have all the features and styling requirements to meet every user's needs, all within most people's budget! These production difficulties are understandable, but it does not lessen the frustration for left-handed users, particularly in digital video camera technology, where single-handed use – but exclusively right-handed – is now the norm.

If using your existing camera equipment is proving particularly difficult for your left-hander, a cordless remote is now a common add-on to many models, allowing control of the basic features with the other hand.

A camera with a centrally located viewfinder.

Sewing, knitting and crochet

Left-handed instruction books on all these crafts are available, but it is often far easier if your child can learn from following another person, rather than from a book. They can usually learn well sitting opposite a right-hander.

Sewing

Left-handers usually work in the opposite direction from a right-hander when sewing, holding the needle in the left hand and positioning the fabric in the right, then working from left to right. If you and your child sit opposite each other, she can more easily imitate what you are doing but the other way around. Regular tacking or running stitch seldom present problems, but this 'mirror image' way of working is especially helpful with more complicated work such as some embroidery stitches.

A good quality pair of left-handed dressmaking and embroidery scissors are essential items in your child's sewing box, and she will probably find a left-handed measuring tape useful, as the measurements run in the more natural right-to-left direction. See Resources (pages 122–123).

Knitting

Right-handers often get in a tangle (sometimes literally) trying to teach a left-hander how to knit. But because this is less emphatically a one-handed action than sewing or crochet, left-handers often knit exactly like right-handers, so is worth seeing whether or not your child runs into difficulties before doing any 'translating'.

Learning to knit left-handed from instructions aimed at right-handers can prove a muddling and confusing experience, so if your child is not to be put off, it is worth finding left-handed instruction (see Resources, pages 122–123) or, even better,

Sewing machines

Sewing machines are normally quite adaptable for left-handers, although the foot pedal may need to be repositioned for a left-footer. The left/right clash comes with sewing pinned fabric. Tacking pins put in by a left-hander will be inclined to run in the opposite direction, which can make it awkward to take them out as the work runs through the machine. There are three ways round this:

- Position the item the other way round so it runs through the middle gap of the machine rather than spreading out to the left. This is an easy alternative for something narrow, such as a belt or small clothes for a baby or a toy doll.

- Adopt the admirable but often bypassed practice of always tacking or basting together two pieces of fabric before machine-sewing them.

- Work out which way round the pins need to be put in to be easy to take out (something most – but not all – right-handers do by instinct), and position yourself in relation to the fabric to achieve this as you pin. (When practicable, pinning crossways, rather than parallel to the cut edges, makes this easier, as you then just need to know to have the pinhead nearest the edge.

If you are right-handed, sit opposite your child so your actions are automatically reversed for her to copy.

demonstrate while sitting opposite each other, to provide a mirror image to follow. Knitting patterns can be used by left- or right-handers, so once children have mastered the basic stitches they are ready to go.

Crochet

A crochet hook can be used equally easily in either hand, so, again, a few sessions with your child following your mirror image manoeuvres should provide the basic know-how. *Crochet Unravelled* (see Resources, pages 122–123) helpfully gives step-by-step illustrations for left- and right-handed working side by side.

Crochet patterns that use the international symbols can easily be followed by left-handers, who simply follow the symbols round clockwise rather than anticlockwise.

Knots, ties and shoelaces

Learning to tie knots and bows can be a struggle for any little one, but particularly for a left-hander as he will have to reverse the instructions you give him if you are not left-handed yourself. If you're a right-hander teaching a left-hander, sit opposite each other rather than side by side, so the left-hander gets a mirror image of what you do. This works for tying knots and ties as well as shoelaces.

Tying shoelaces

Most children do not learn to tie shoelaces until about five or six years old, with girls usually more adept at it than boys. It is quite a hard skill to master requiring a great deal of patience from both the child and the person teaching them!

Left-handers tie the opposite way to right-handers.

A knotty problem

It is helpful to teach your child to tie simple knots, for example ribbons, neck ties and shoelaces, in a mirror image to the right-handed way (see opposite), as this is more comfortable for him and these are likely to be the knots he uses predominantly in his daily life. However, older children may develop hobbies that require them to learn tying complicated, specialist knots, such as those used in sailing or mountaineering. For strength and security it is obviously extremely important to get these knots right.

Since instructions are normally written for right-handers, left-handers are usually advised to learn the right-handed way for a number of reasons. Firstly, it saves having to reverse references to 'right' and 'left' when using instruction manuals, which can be extremely confusing. It is important to tie knots correctly – carelessly taking the working end over where it should go under, or vice versa can result in a different knot, or sometimes no knot at all. And of course, there are safety considerations as a result of the conventions involved in working in a team with other people.

Left- and right-handed knots

It is worth being aware that some basic knots can be classified as left- or right-handed. In fact this has nothing to do with whether the person tying them is left- or right-handed!

By way of example, a simple overhand knot is classified as right-handed or left-handed if the two entwined knotted parts spiral or helix towards the right (clockwise), or towards the left (anticlockwise).

Tying a shoelace

There are lots of ways of tying shoelaces, but here is one simple way your child can try.

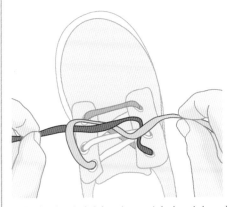

1 Curl string in left hand over right hand thread, under and pull through.

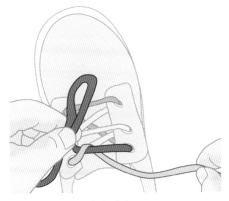

2 Make a loop and pinch it.

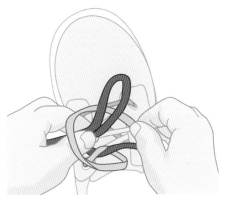

3 Curl thread in right hand around loop.

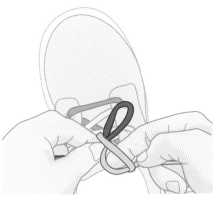

4 Push thread in right hand under itself to make new loop.

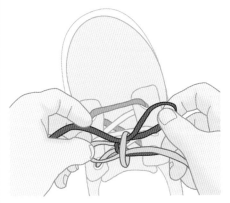

5 Hold new loop with left hand and old loop with right.

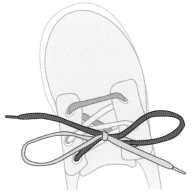

6 Pull loops tight to make your bow!

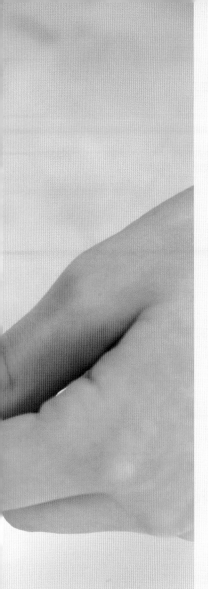

Left-handedness and School

Life in the classroom

The school years should be an exciting time for your child, who will encounter new challenges and experiences every day. Hopefully, you will have helped your child have the confidence to try out new skills and to question any technique or tool that does not work efficiently and comfortably.

How teachers can make a difference

Unfortunately, you should not assume that your child's school is aware of how best to address left-handers' needs. Your child's teachers will undoubtedly be trained in and supportive of a wide range of social, cultural and developmental issues but left-handedness is unlikely to be one of them.

Teacher training courses do not usually cover the subject of teaching left-handed students, so new teachers routinely enter the profession totally unaware that left-handers may even . experience any difficulties, let alone how to combat them. Experienced teachers may develop their own individual approach to helping their left-handed pupils (ranging in effectiveness from excellent to cursory) or dismiss any issues relating to handedness as insignificant. The frustration here is that the needs of left-handers are so simply met and easy to teach.

The attitude towards left-handers has improved considerably in recent years, and continues to do so. Many teachers are wonderfully supportive and keen to find out how best to help their left-handed pupils once they are made aware of the issues that need to be addressed, and will do all they can to ensure these children receive equal and relevant training in essential skills such as handwriting. The outright discrimination against left-handers that was the accepted attitude in the past has now largely gone (although some cultures still consider the left hand to be 'unclean') and the important distinction now is that children are allowed to write with their left hand but are *not always shown the best way to do so*.

Often, teachers are confident that they are doing all that is necessary to help their left-handers, yet on closer inspection are totally unaware that there are different basic handwriting skills for left-handers, or that positioning of students within the classroom is important. Dishearteningly, many are aware that left-handers need left-handed scissors, but have invested in so-called 'ambidextrous' scissors from educational suppliers who advertise them as equally suitable for left and right-handed use when they are nothing of the sort (see page 62). For many schools, this is where they consider their responsibility towards their left-handed students starts and ends. Ironically, left-handed teachers can sometimes be the worst culprits, as they quite naturally assume they know how every left-hander functions. But, as we have seen in Chapter 1, there are so many degrees of hand dominance and preference that children should have their own individual challenges actively addressed, as one may be more or less capable of adapting skills than a left-handed classmate.

How you can make a difference

Your child may be wonderfully adaptable, and the confidence and skills you give her in her early years will pay great dividends in her approach to overcoming new hurdles in her school life, so there is every chance she will progress through school without her handedness ever becoming an issue, as thousands of left-handers do every day. Knowing the potential hurdles means you and your child are forewarned in case of difficulties, and ready to address any concerns with the school if they arise, in a positive, informed and constructive manner.

Teachers are sometimes unaware of the specific needs of their left-handed pupils.

It is to be hoped that all teachers would welcome suggestions to improve the classroom layout or teaching techniques for their pupils' benefit, but this is often not the case – and a great degree of tact is needed when trying to tell a teacher how to do his or her job! To be fair, it is unrealistic to expect a school to change its whole policy, layout and range of equipment overnight, at the behest of one child who may not even have started studying subjects in some of the areas that need addressing! It is best to establish a friendly and positive relationship with the staff, and an active interest in the development of the school, perhaps by joining the PTA. Deal with issues as your child progresses through the school, and encourage other parents to do the same. Where you do find problems, however, be resolute that improvements must be made. Your child has just as much right to equal and relevant learning as right-handed students.

Support in the classroom

If your child is struggling with a concept or new skill that everyone else seems to be finding quite straightforward, he should have the awareness and confidence to question whether a right-hand bias may be the cause. The teacher should be positive and supportive, and work with the child to find a more convenient or comfortable way of working.

Your child's school environment should be adapted.

Helping left-handed students

Left-handed children have an equal right to receive the correct basic training and equipment that will enable them to reach their full potential in all subjects, yet many struggle needlessly. Teachers are often unaware of the hindrances that can make some subjects more awkward for left-handed students. For example, in a recent study by the Left-Handers' Association, of left-handers under 25 years of age who had been in full-time education, nearly all (99 per cent) had experienced difficulty with their handwriting, yet only 10 per cent had received specific guidance on left-handed writing techniques from their teachers. Opposite is some further information that emerged from the same study.

The overwhelming message from this survey is that there is a significant gap in teachers' knowledge relating to their left-handed pupils. Far too few teachers are aware of their left-handed students' needs and, crucially, do not know how easily these needs can be met. This is a matter of great concern.

Training

There is obviously an urgent need to provide teachers with information about the simple but effective steps that can overcome the majority of frustrations left-handed students encounter. Left-handedness need never be a problem for children provided teachers can guide them in the techniques to adopt when approaching new tasks as a left-hander. The Resources section (pages 122–123) contains a lot of useful guidance for both parents and teachers.

Survey results from the Left-Handers' Association

Writing
Despite teaching aids specifically for left-handed children now being easily available via specialist websites, only 3 per cent of students had specific writing practice mats/word formation exercises for left-handed writing. Most worryingly, a startling 85 per cent had never been taught the best posture and paper positioning for writing left-handed. This basic training is essential, particularly since 76 per cent of students complained of backache or hand fatigue when writing, due to a poor writing style.

Smudging is a common problem for left-handers, with over 88 per cent experiencing this problem, yet only 7 per cent had ever been given guidance on improving their hand position to eliminate smudging.

Although writing is the most obvious area of difficulty for left-handers the survey highlights causes for concern in many areas of the curriculum. The main issues are:

Equipment
Left-handers routinely struggle with right-hand- biased equipment but are not given advice on how to adapt safely and efficiently, nor given the option of left-handed versions. Common responses were 'Not cost-effective to provide specialized equipment for such a small group' and 'learn to cut with your other hand'.

Safety
Older children using power tools in DT/woodwork/metalwork that are designed for the safety of right-handed users routinely work at awkward angles, and with insufficient access to safety features.

Consideration
Few students felt teachers noticed they were left-handed or checked that they could use the tools or equipment in a comfortable and safe way. Shared workstations were always set up for right-handers' convenience, despite 41 per cent of left-handers finding this inefficient. Worryingly, many left-handers do not feel that teachers consider their difficulties to be valid.

Equality of teaching
There is no specific teaching of left-handed techniques in the vast majority of subjects, despite a huge proportion of left-handers finding tasks awkward. Writing, DT, textiles, sports, food technology, IT and music were particularly highlighted.

Teacher training
A number of trainee teachers completed the survey, and reported that they have received no training whatsoever in how to help left-handed students.

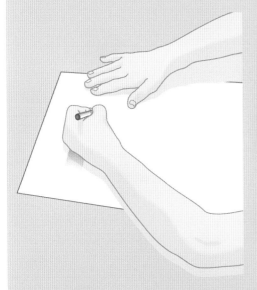

A poor writing style is a common problem.

Special learning requirements

Studies show an unexpectedly high number of left-handers in certain groups of extremely bright individuals, and it is often suggested that left-handedness is a common trait among children with specific learning requirements. This may well be a by-product of their preference for right-brain thinking.

Gifted children

If you have a highly intelligent child, you will be well aware of the difficulty of trying to find games that will engage his interest and attention for more than a few minutes. Your left-handed child may well question conventional rules of learning (such as rote learning of times tables) and sometimes a fresh approach to practising basic skills will appeal to them. (See All in the mind? in Chapter 1, page 18).

Dyslexia and discalculia

There has also been much speculation that a higher proportion of dyslexic children are left-

Left-handers respond well to visual and auditory learning techniques.

handed. Many people's experience would tend to agree with this, but there has yet to be a conclusive study to confirm it, and since most schools do not note the handedness of their pupils as a matter of course, it is not an easy matter to determine.

Often, a specific learning difficulty can hinder an otherwise exceptionally able child and that difficulty can overshadow their many talents. The ability of a dyslexic child for 3-D imagery, for instance, may leave other children standing! Toys and games that play to their strengths, while encouraging practice of more difficult areas greatly increase their confidence and self-esteem (see Chapter 3, pages 46–47).

Dyscalculia is a condition where children have difficulty in arithmetic, particularly in speed and fluency of simple calculations, although mathematical ability may be high. Often, these children cannot represent calculations on paper even though they are able to carry them out. Play games that address some common difficulties, which include slowness in calculations, memorizing multiplication tables, directional difficulties and poor short-term memory.

ADD/ADHD

Attention deficit disorder (ADD) and attention deficit hyperactive disorder (ADHD) often co-exist with dyslexia. ADD children display poor attention span and are easily distracted, leading to daydreaming and switching off. They may be restless and fidgety, its more extreme form being hyperactivity. They tend to be impetuous or impulsive, acting without thinking and are poor planners. They fit into the category of clumsy child and have poor coordination for fine motor skills such as tying shoelaces and legible handwriting. Formal learning situations can be difficult, so try to make tasks fun and relaxed. Games that provide a quick reward, and group activities that don't require them to 'wait their turn' are often the most rewarding. Highly complex and intricate puzzles are also worth considering for some ADD children, who can often find them totally absorbing, while improving their hand–eye coordination and fine motor skills at the same time.

Always investigate further if your child is struggling.

Learning difficulties

While incidence of left-handedness, cross-laterality (opposite hand and eye being dominant) or undetermined handedness is higher among people with some learning difficulties, it is important to stress that left-handedness does not *cause* learning difficulties or disabilities (e.g. dyslexia, dyspraxia, dyscalculia, ADD/ADHD) although it may occur in addition to them. Left-handers face practical challenges with tools and positioning, but if your child is having learning difficulties it is unlikely to be because he is left-handed, so always look further for an underlying cause.

Right-brain learning

Because of the dominance of their right brain, the visual and creative hemisphere, many left-handers assimilate information far better when given visual and tactile references and explanations.

Learning styles

We all absorb information from the world around us in three basic ways, by looking (visual), listening (auditory) and feeling (kinaesthetic). Although we use all of these skills every day, most of us are more receptive to one style over the others. This style forms our most effective method of communicating and learning.

The traditional style of teaching, a classroom lecture with very few pictures/diagrams, is not always as effective for visual and kinaesthetic learners. This is why the best teachers are those who incorporate all styles into their teaching and vary their language to include phrases such as:

'You will see that....', 'We will get to grips with...', 'Listen to this....' , 'I feel that .....', to appeal to everyone in a group. Games and activities should ideally be multi-sensory, to give children opportunities to look at and take part in activities as well as listen.

Knowing which style your left-handed child prefers, and using it to communicate with her can vastly improve her understanding and can often resolve frustration or conflicts caused by trying to make a point in your own preferred style if this is different (for example, using an auditory approach to someone who understands best through visual information).

Try experimenting with different educational games and activities to discover your child's learning style.

Visual, auditory or kinaesthetic?

To establish which style of learning your child prefers, ask the following simple questions. The answers indicate a leaning towards a visual (V), auditory (A) or kinaesthetic (K) style of learning.

When you are learning your times tables, how do you remember the answers?
- You look, then cover over the tables and try to picture them. (V)
- You say the tables out loud. (A)
- You use your fingers or hands to help. (K)

You have a list of spellings to learn. What do you do?
- You say each letter out loud again and again. (A)
- You write the words over and over again. (K)
- You look hard at each word and remember what it looks like. (V)

In a history lesson you are learning new facts. Which way is best for you?
- Watching a video. (V)
- Listening to a tape or radio programme explaining what happened. (A)
- Taking part in a role-play and acting out what happened. (K)

You want to find out how an alarm clock works. What do you do?
- You take the object apart then put it back together again. (K)
- You look at a diagram or a picture. (V)
- You listen to a teacher telling you about it. (A)

You have made a cake before, with help. This time you want to do it on you own. How do you do it?
- You follow a recipe. (V)
- You ask someone to tell you what to do. (A)
- You just get started and remember what to do as you go along. (K)

You are learning to count in another language. What is best for you?
- Singing the words. (A)
- Looking at cards and posters. (V)
- Playing a game with the words. (K)

If you have to learn a list of facts in order, which is easiest?
- You act or dance them in a sequence. (K)
- You read over the list several times. (V)
- You make up a song or a rhyme. (A)

Multi-sensory back-up

Look out for educational games that use an alternative approach to learning important skills. Card games that use the times tables have proved hugely popular with many left-handers and greatly improved their times tables skills. Board games based on the school curriculum for learning a foreign language are a bright, lively alternative way to learn some of the most useful phrases your child (and you!) will need, as you speak, listen and play together.

Mind Maps are a highly visual and creative study aid that are said to appeal to right-brain thinkers. Widely supported in schools and colleges, mind-mapping was championed by Tony Buzan, who recognized the potential of tapping into right-brain thinking to increase learning ability and encourage lateral thinking. Students draw image-based diagrams to represent connections between pieces of information relating to one overall topic, in a radial, non-linear manner, using colourful images and words that are easy to memorize and understand.

Mind Maps are an excellent way to harness creativity and preference for thinking in pictures to create study aids and organizational tools that the left-hander will enjoy creating and using. See Resources, pages 122–123, for more information.

Using school equipment

One of the most enduring and widespread obstacles is the overwhelming lack of awareness of the difficulties that can be created for left-handers expected to perform seemingly simple and straightforward tasks but in a position or with equipment that is totally biased against them.

Raising awareness

It is important for schools to be aware of the areas of nuisance or difficulty for a left-hander, but also crucial that these differences are not treated as an oddity or an inconvenience within the class. A good teacher, once aware of them, will simply and casually adopt any measures that ensure the most efficient and comfortable way of working, as a standard part of the teaching process. If a child feels embarrassed or singled out, his desire to fit back in will override any interest in working more effectively, and he will probably fight any suggestions, however helpful.

Whiteboards/blackboards

Left-handers can be encouraged to improve their standard writing technique by using the class whiteboard. This enables them to use the larger muscles in the arm, relax the shoulder and alleviate tension that can build up when huddled over a desk. If hand position needs correcting, the left hand will be following the writing before the marker has dried, so work on the whiteboard is frequently turned into streaks or smudges. This can be solved by practising the following:

- Holding the marker/chalk further back from the tip, so they don't rest their hand on the board as they write
- Using a larger, more relaxed style, using the whole arm from the shoulder keeping the hand under the writing line at all times. (This may require them to write higher up the board at first, well above their shoulder.)
- Start writing well to the left of their body rather than directly in front of them, as this brings the hand underneath the writing and they are now pulling the marker/chalk towards them as they write, so the hand is no longer following the work and cannot smudge it.

Sloped writing board

Writing boards that slope at an angle of approximately 20 degrees are a great help in preventing or correcting a hooked writing position or bad posture. They encourage children to sit in a more upright position, with a good line of sight to their work, and enable them to write without stretching the shoulders or craning the neck.

Writing boards are readily available – your child's school may already have some, as they are also helpful for right-handers. As the surface can sometimes be rather hard, a writing mat or pad of paper under the workbook can make writing more comfortable.

Spiral notebooks and ring-binders

Traditionally, a new clean page is always the one on the right side of an open book or folder. For left-handers this often means a constant and uncomfortable obstacle of the spiral bound spine

Did you know?

When thumbing through a book or magazine, left-handers generally start at the back of the magazine, and thumb through to the front. It often feels more natural to work in this direction.

or the ring binding directly beneath their left hand and arm. This can be a constant nuisance, making writing awkward and uncomfortable, and forcing them to abandon the ideal left-handed writing position to seek a comfortable position for themselves and their notebooks. There are some simple adaptations that can help to overcome this problem.

Try using notebooks spiral bound at the top rather than the side, or start at the back of the book and work towards the front.

A ring-binder with a standard hole-punched, lined pad and margin can be easily adapted for left-hand use by tearing off the back sheet or cardboard backing and starting on the back page. This way, the margin is still on the left of the pages, but the rings are on the right, well out of the way.

If your child is changing the way he organizes his workbooks, make sure the reasons are explained to the teacher so it is not just seen as 'awkward' behaviour.

Workbooks and test papers

Assuming left-handed children have their writing paper properly positioned on the desk, they may find it easier to copy from workbooks placed to the right of their work. When completing worksheets that have questions on the left side and space for writing answers on the right, however, left-handers will either be routinely covering up the questions, or the text will be too far away to their left to be read comfortably. A photocopy of the printed page or an additional copy of the book that can be placed to the right of their written work may help.

This is a very real problem when completing 'multiple choice' or 'bubble' tests, where the questions are answered by ticking a box or blacking out a circle in a column located to the right of the question. Again, left-handers will be disadvantaged as they will have to repeatedly move position to uncover the next question. If the test is being timed, this will almost certainly cost them valuable time and create unnecessary stress. An additional copy of the questions can be placed to the right side of the answer column, but great care must be taken to ensure the questions line up exactly with the answers, as a shift by even one line may be disastrous.

Scissors

If there is one tool that every left-handed child should have access to, it is left-handed scissors, and schools are notoriously lax in providing enough of these. Many schools are now misguidedly stocking 'universal' scissors in their classrooms, having been led to believe that they are fine for left-handers to use. They are not. For why not, and why left-handed scissors are needed, see page 62.

Avoid knocking elbows – seat left-handers to the left.

Positioning within the classroom

This is often something that teachers are quite unaware of until it is brought (tactfully) to their attention. The most obvious precaution is, in a classroom with shared desks, not to seat a right-hander to the left of a left-hander, as they will immediately knock elbows when they start writing. As well as being an excuse for a distraction, this usually results in the left-hander turning sideways on to the desk, resulting in dreadful posture, inefficient writing and eventually, the 'hooked' writing position so commonly associated with left-handed writers. There are three simple solutions for the teacher:

- Ask the two pupils to swap places

- Seat left-handers next to each other

- If seated in rows, place the left-handers on the left end of the row.

Even with individual desks some positions within the classroom are disadvantageous to left-handers. When they are in the correct writing position it is more awkward to look to the right to see the board, and this can become a strain when doing a lot of copying. Ideally, they should be somewhere in the right half of the room (presuming the board is central on the front wall), where they can glance at the board without any change in writing position.

It is also good for teachers to be alert to any position where a left-hander's body or hand may block a light source that would fall uninterrupted on to a right-hander's work.

Rulers

The measurements on a ruler run from left to right, so a right-hander can pull a pencil or pen along the edge, creating a uniform, well-defined line while clearly seeing the measurement progress. A left-hander, however, has to push from the left, restricting the ink flow or blunting the lead, so the line is thicker at the end than it was at the beginning. Young children may even catch or tear the paper. To overcome this, left-handers often draw lines 'back to front', from right to left. This is fine for general underlining, but is more awkward for specific measurements.

For example, in order to accurately measure from, say 0 to 8 (whether it's centimetres or inches), they find it more natural to start at the 8 mark and pull the pencil towards the 0. However, although they can see the 8 mark to start the line, their hand now obscures the left side of the ruler and they cannot see the measurements to gauge where 0 is, or even the end of the ruler! They regularly overshoot the end slightly, resulting in a 'dogleg' end to lines where they have drawn round the end of the ruler.

The solution is to use a left-handed ruler, which has the measurements running from right to left.

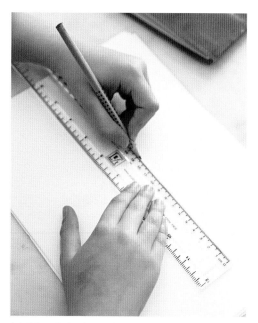

A left-handed ruler with reversed measurements.

A left-handed sharpener works anticlockwise.

Chairs with hinged writing tablets

One of the most common causes of backache and bad posture is the necessity for left-handers to sit at chairs in class that have the writing tablet attached to the right side of the chair. By their very nature, the fact that they are so comfortable for right-handers to use makes them extremely uncomfortable and impractical for left-handers. These chairs provide no support for the left arm, leading to stress in the arm and shoulder muscles, and consequently poor writing style. The left-handed pupil is forced to adopt a twisted, slouching posture in order to achieve some level of support at the desk and enable her to write.

Desks with left-handed writing tablets are widely available from school furniture suppliers. Schools may need to be encouraged to ensure they know how many left-handed students will be attending before every class, and make sure they each have a left-handed workstation. If the school does not have enough, there should be no question that more are ordered.

Using a ruler such as this, a pen or pencil can be pulled towards the left hand with complete control, and the measurements remain clearly visible at all times.

If left-handed rulers, protractors and so on are not available to your child, it is sometimes easier to turn the workbook sideways so the measure is running from top to bottom, and then draw the line vertically, with the hand to the left side of the measurement.

Pencil sharpeners

A pencil sharpener is designed so that the blade engages as the pencil is turned away from the body when held in the right hand. When turned round for a pencil to be inserted from the left side, the blade is now reversed, and the pencil has to be turned towards the body – a far less comfortable and efficient action, giving less grip and control. The resulting shavings now emerge towards the body of a left-hander, falling down her front or into her lap!

A left-handed sharpener has the blade on the opposite side, so a left-hander can push the pencil away from the body, and the shavings can be easily directed towards the bin.

Poor pupil!

A left-hander turns up to class to find only chairs with right-handed writing tablets. She is told there are definitely some left-handed chairs 'somewhere in the building' and is sent off to search. The rest of the class, meanwhile, continues the lesson. Not only is this a huge waste of the poor pupil's valuable study time, but it causes her great embarrassment. As a result, next time she slides into a right-handed desk, with assurances that 'this is OK, I'll be fine here'. She never asks for a suitable desk again, and her work, handwriting and back suffer the consequences.

It is the school's responsibility to provide equal and adequate workstations for each child and the onus should not be on any child to beg for one.

Top tips for schoolchildren

Starting at school is a major step in your child's life, and he will probably approach it with a mixture of excitement and uncertainty. These years are crucial for developing confidence, self-esteem, and social and learning skills so a positive approach is essential.

Tools for school

A few simple items will make a huge difference to your child's progress in writing and cutting. Check whether the school provide these items but if not, it is definitely worth investing in them for use both at school and home.

- Oversized 'tri-grip' pens and pencils
- Left-handed pencil grip
- Left-handers' writing mat (showing correct positioning and letter formations)
- Fully left-handed scissors (if you provide your own, make sure they are clearly labelled and within easy reach when your child needs them). (See Using scissors, pages 60–61).

Once your child progresses to ink pens, choose an ergonomic left-handed grip for better control, and a left-handed fountain pen with a specially chamfered nib.

Be aware of the other left-handed items available (see Resources, pages 122–123) but let your child try using regular ones first, and see how he manages.

Handwriting

Handwriting is the most conspicuous problem your left-hander will have to tackle as he will have to work harder to write legibly, so it may take longer to complete tasks or assignments.

Encourage your child to use standard school equipment and adapt where necessary. Try both sides of his body for new skills as he may not be left-dominant for everything – versatility is one of the blessings of left-handedness!

Make sure the teacher allows for this. Follow the tips for good writing on page 54.

Desk positioning

To avoid knocking elbows and cramped desk space, your left-hander should always sit on the left side of a double desk, at the left end of a row, or next to another left-hander. The teacher should ensure there is enough room on the left of the desk space to allow a left-hander to position his paper slightly to the side. If chairs with hinged writing tablets are used, the school should ensure there are enough left-handed versions for all the left-handers in the class.

Materials

In science, art and cookery classes, it is safer and more convenient for a left-hander to keep chemicals, materials and ingredients to his left. When working in pairs, he should always stand to the left to avoid knocking elbows.

Electrical equipment

When first using electrical equipment in woodwork, metalwork or textiles, the teacher should make sure that your child is able to access any safety features with his left hand in case of an emergency. Children should also feel totally comfortable and fully in control of the equipment with their stronger hand (whether left or right) before using it unsupervised.

Computers

If your child has greater control over the computer mouse in his left hand, ask the IT department to designate a computer with a left-handed mouse, or download mouse swapping software to the desktop so he can change the buttons and cursor round easily.

Workbooks and binders

If the binding on ring-binders and spiral bound pads make note-taking uncomfortable, your child could try making Mind Maps (see page 83), with the notebook turned landscape. This gets the binding up and out of the way, and will allow him to work in a visual and creative way that appeals to left-handers, and can be much faster than handwriting.

Where printed workbooks or test papers have questions on the left and answer space on the right, your left-hander's hand and arm may cover the questions, or they may be too far to the left for him to read. Your child may find it helps to position a second book/sheet containing the questions on the right of his answer space, directly in front of him.

First school days

Dealing with frustration Your child is likely to be presented with lots of new toys and equipment, some of which he may find more awkward to use than his classmates. Naturally this can be frustrating, but it will stand him in good stead for future years if he can learn to deal with situations calmly, and persevere rather than lose his temper or avoid the task. Encourage him to think round the problem, and work with his teacher to find a method, or equipment that works best for him.

Note If mirror writing, difficulty with fine manipulation or an inability to write continues after age six it may be a sign of possible neurodevelopmental problems, learning difficulty or a visual impairment and your child's school may advise assessment for these different conditions.

Talking with your child's teacher Try to develop a good relationship with your child's teacher early on. Let her know your child is left-handed and find out what strategies she has that could help a left-hander if he is struggling, but do not make a big issue of it. If your child is undecided about his handedness when he starts school, ask that he be encouraged to use both hands for tasks whilst he works out which feels more comfortable. Boys develop fine motor skills later than girls, so may take longer to decide. Do not intervene in your child's schooling unless there is real concern, and be tactful if you make suggestions.

Handwriting

Left-handers need to learn some simple but basic writing techniques that are quite different from those right-handers apply. It is therefore essential that your child receives specific instruction on how to approach writing as a left-hander, and is not made to follow the techniques taught to his right-handed classmates or, equally wrongly, left to 'work it out for himself'.

A good writing style learned from an early age makes the transition to ink pens much easier.

Back to basics

It is comparatively easy to teach young schoolchildren the correct writing style, as they enjoy the rhythmic movement of creating letters and have not had any setbacks to create tension (see pages 40–43 for setting the groundwork for a good writing style).

Many children do not experience difficulties until they start using ink pens, when a poor grip causes smudging, or even later, when they are taking lots of notes, when poor posture and a slow writing style lead to tension, backache and aching hands. If your child has started formal writing and is having difficulties, it is usually best to go back to the basics of handwriting (see pages 92–93), alleviate tension and stress, and try to create in your child a positive attitude to writing, where he sees lots of achievement and progress.

Overcoming 'muscle memory'

If your child has been writing for some time, he will find the new positioning you are encouraging strange and possible a bit awkward, which may sound ridiculous if you are correcting a severely hooked hand and hunched writing posture! But all of us, when repeating tasks on a regular basis, develop a 'muscle memory' where our body, after a while, automatically assumes the position we have always used to perform a task, and writing is no different. When a child has learned to form letters with his hand in a certain position, it will be hard for his body and brain to accept doing it in a different way. Consequently, while he improves posture, grip and paper position, his writing will at first appear more juvenile and poorly formed, and the effort to form the letters will seem greater. Always reassure him that this is perfectly natural, and will quickly pass.

As he learns the new techniques and uses them regularly, he will very quickly regain the speed and control he had before, and then continue to improve in leaps and bounds. A few school days of diligently using the new positioning for all lessons should be all that's needed to make him feel comfortable.

Do make sure that all teachers are aware that your child is practising to improve his writing style, so they can make allowances if his written

Softly, softly

When first working with a child who has handwriting difficulties, I start by asking them to show me how they write, and make sure I praise something about their current writing they do well. After a brief chat to put them at ease, possibly comparing the way we form letters, or which pens we like to use, I then share with them a trick I know to make the smudging disappear (or whatever the problem is) and they can see that by following my advice, the problem often goes away!

A perfect writing position with an ergonomic pen.

work appears less neat for a few days, and can also remind him to adopt the correct writing position if he forgets – old habits die hard! Don't make your child feel he is being 'corrected' for writing in a different style, and never force him to write or draw if he doesn't feel inclined, or it will feel like a chore.

Basic writing shapes and forms

The simple patterns that form the basis of fluent handwriting can be used at any stage of learning or improvement, from beginners through to adults wishing to improve their speed and legibility.

Basic patterns

The basic patterns below are rhythmic repetitions that can be practised in normal size, or larger on a whiteboard or easel. Get your child to concentrate on the rhythm and fluency, so the writing becomes relaxed and fluid.

UUUUUUUUUUUU
1 Swing under

mmmmmmmmmmm
2 Arches

llllllll
3 Loops

CCCCCCCCC
4 Waves

CUCUCUCUCU
5 Combining patterns 1 and 4

VVVVVVVVVV
6 Zig-zags

Letter formation

When it comes to forming letters, left-handers form a few letters in a slightly different way (see opposite). As you can see, the main difference is in the horizontal crosses on letters, which left-handers form from right to left because there is

School policy

Although most schools adopt a particular writing style that all children must adhere to, they should also have a policy on helping left-handers, so will be happy to adopt these very slight amendments to writing style that will ease the left-handers' progress.

less resistance when 'pulling' to draw the line rather than pushing.

This becomes even more obvious when progressing to a cartridge pen, where the ink flow is interrupted and the nib catches when the pen is pushed. The letter 'O' is also sometimes written anticlockwise.

It is advisable to include these different strokes into the form of writing your child learns (usually cursive), as they are easier to incorporate once your child progresses to a cartridge pen, and feel far more comfortable.

Learning word spacing

Young children are often taught to get even spacing between words by measuring a finger width. Right-handed children can place their left forefinger after the last word written, but this does not work for left-handers, as placing their right forefinger after the last word would obstruct the line. A simple alternative is to suggest leaving the space of an imaginary letter 'o' before starting the next word.

Differing left-handed letter formation

The horizontal lines are formed differently in capital 'A', 'F', 'G', 'H', 'I', 'J' and 'T'.

Horizontal lines are also formed differently in lowercase 'f' and 't'.

Common handwriting problems

Many children have difficulties of one sort or another with writing well and easily. The problems that occur most often among left-handers usually stem from the inherent difficulty with writing 'unnaturally' from left to right.

'Hook' handwriting position

This is where the hand is hooked around the pen, and runs above the writing line in an attempt to angle the pen in the same way as a right-hander would. This causes the arm and body to be contorted into an awkward position, making handwriting very uncomfortable and slow. Relearning the correct position for hand and paper (see page 91) may take a little while, but will reap benefits. Ensure that the desk/table and chair are a suitable height for the child. A low table makes a child raise his shoulders, which can encourage hunching and bending in the 'hooked' style – a sloped writing board helps prevent this.

A cramped grip causes tension and smudging.

Smudged work

Work gets smudged because the hand pushing the pen across the page is running over newly written work. It is often because of experience with smudging that left-handers then graduate to the 'hook' position in an effort to keep their hand clear of what they have just written. Instead, the correct hand position keeps the hand *below* the written line (see pages 56–57).

Overtight grip

This leads to cramped, badly formed letters and an erratic writing style and is also very tiring. It is caused by a number of related factors:

- **Bad desk positioning** If a left-hander is seated with a right-hander on his left they will knock arms. This will force both of them to write in a restricted space. See page 86 for suggestions that avoid this.
- **Tension because of concern about handwriting** Praise and reassurance as he relearns a better position and style help here.
- **The wrong pen** A slippery or shiny pen barrel is hard to hold. Make sure the pen/pencil is comfortable to grip without undue pressure, especially when hands are hot or tired. A pencil grip is also helpful (see page 58).

Mirror writing

Reversing letters and numbers is very common among young children. For left-handers in particular, when they are first learning to write, the natural inclination is to start at the right of the page and move towards the left, pulling the pencil towards their body and enabling them to see what they have written without their hand getting in the way. Mirror writers often produce

Difficulties with arm angle and grip

The angle of the child's writing arm can range through almost 180 degrees. Many of the positions left-handers adopt are very cramped and the so-called 'hooked' grip is especially awkward. Although many children seem to get by well enough with these unusual positions, they can lead to problems such as neck and shoulder pain.

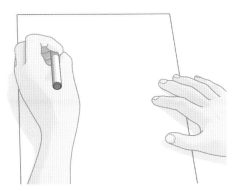

In the straight position left-handers find it hard to see what they are writing, unless they lean forward.

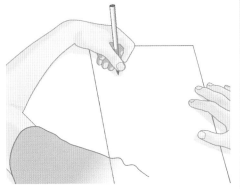

The hooked position offers a good view but is awkward and uncomfortable.

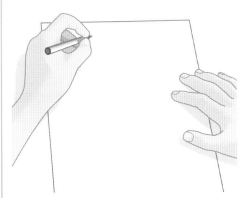

Here, the angled position of the wrist affords the left-hander a better view but it may be uncomfortable.

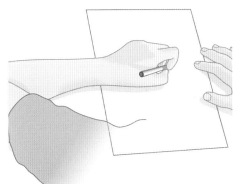

The horizontal position is difficult to maintain and visibility is impaired.

perfect reverse script, which can be read clearly if viewed in a mirror. (Leonardo da Vinci was left-handed and a famously perfect mirror writer, as was Lewis Carroll.)

Children should never be chastised for this, just gently corrected, as it is perfectly normal and usually stops once they become accustomed to the direction of reading and writing. Putting a coloured sticker or drawing a star at the top left margin can help remind your child where to start writing on new blank sheets of paper.

If mirror writing continues after about six years old, it may be a sign of an underlying learning difficulty, so consult your child's teacher.

Right-handed bias in classes

Although budgets and ingrained habit play their part, right-handed bias in the classroom, laboratory or school workshops is most often because of lack of awareness on the school's part. The following notes may help iron out many problems if brought to the attention of the teacher or school.

Food technology

Certain commonly used kitchen tools are designed specifically for right-handed use (see box below), and left-handers will not be able to work as efficiently or comfortably, or in some cases as safely, with these items. However, properly designed left-handed versions of all commonly used kitchen implements are available (see Resources, pages 122–123).

Another common difficulty is kettles or hobs positioned inconveniently so left-handers cannot pour/stir/cook comfortably. Controls on cookers, hobs and microwaves are often positioned on the right side, forcing left-handers (who usually hold the pan handle or bowl in their right hand, and keep their left free to stir) to reach across the stove to work the controls. Most manufacturers produce hobs with controls at the front, which are much safer for a left-hander.

Science

Remember that left-handers will pour and stir with their left hand so for safety all chemicals should be placed to their left.

Chemical equipment, much like kitchen equipment, is designed for right-handed use.

- Pouring lips on crucibles are often placed so they can only be used when poured from the right hand.
- Scalpels with a sharpened edge on the left side of the blade (when held ready to cut) will tend to curve inwards for a left-hander so do not give an accurate cut. Ideally, the blade should be sharpened on both sides of the cutting edge to give better control.
- Chemical beakers and measuring jugs with measurements only printed down one side cannot be read when held by left-handers. Measurements down both sides of the container allow left-handers to read them off as accurately as right-handers.
- On standard microscopes the focus and light adjustment knob are usually on the right-hand side, as are on–off switches for chemical centrifuges and other analysis equipment, forcing left-handers to contort themselves to work the machine.

Kitchen implements that don't work for left-handers

- Vegetable peeler

- Can opener

- Kitchen scissors

- Angled spatula

- Corkscrew

- Serrated kitchen knives

- Milk pans with a single pouring lip on the left, which is on the wrong side for left-hand pouring

- Measuring jugs and electric kettles with increments only on one side (these are not visible when working left-handed)

Equipment should be to the left of the workspace.

they looked at the space surrounding the drawing rather than at the image itself. After studying research on brain hemisphere functions, she developed her theory that drawing ability was linked to the ability to shift from the verbal, analytical left hemisphere (which she calls 'left mode') to the intuitive, spatial and creative right hemisphere ('right mode'). Her teaching method encourages students to access their right hemisphere, performing tasks that only use the 'right mode'. On doing so, Betty Edwards has seen dramatic improvements in their drawing, and even the less promising students produced impressive pieces of artwork.

For left-handed artists who are inclined to smudge their work, pencils with offset lead tips (see page 59) may be an easy solution. Because the grip is removed from the tip of the pencil, there is little chance of the hand smudging newly drawn work.

Left-handed scissors should be available (see page 60), and clearly marked.

As in the classroom, when pupils are working in pairs side by side, the left-hander should always be positioned to the left of a right-hander so they do not knock elbows or cramp each other's workspace.

Art

Left-handers are said to be more creative and artistic, so you may be nurturing a budding Leonardo da Vinci or Michelangelo!

When imagining pictures in our head, everyone uses their 'right brain' (see pages 18–19), but this side is more dominant in left-handers, which is why they are better at thinking in pictures. Indeed, many teachers encourage right-handed artists to try drawing with their left hand, which often stimulates this side of the brain and has interesting results!

Californian art teacher Betty Edwards has documented this technique in her book *Drawing on the Right Side of the Brain* (see Resources, pages 122–123). Ms Edwards noticed that her students produced far better pictures if they copied a drawing that was upside down, or if

If a left-hander holds a paintbrush awkwardly because of a 'hooked' handwriting style, it can be helpful to work standing at an easel for a period and using big, bold strokes. This relaxes the hand and arm, and working at height will encourage the arm to drop back into a comfortable position underneath the brush or pen.

The blade on a craft knife is extremely sharp, so the correct design and a comfortable secure grip in the left hand are absolutely vital. Craft knives with a dual edge can be easily set up before use to work for a left-hander, and the blade position changed for a right-hander if required. (See Other cutting tools, page 64.)

Left-handers will need left-handed scissors for any art or craft work that requires cutting out – masterpieces might be ruined if they cannot cut accurately! See Using scissors, page 60).

Many art and craft implements with a right-handed bias are also available in left-handed forms: see Resources, pages 122–123.

Information technology

For left-handers who are not adept at using a mouse right-handed, the facility to swap mice positions and functions easily is simple to set up (see page 68) but will help left-mousers a great deal.

Heavy machinery and tools

Safety is a particular concern when it comes to operating larger equipment and more complex tools, such as those in woodwork, metalwork and design technology workshops. Often, just taking the left-handers' existence into account can lead to some fairly simple solutions to increase safety and comfort for left-handers – without, of course, compromising the working conditions for right-handers!

Workshop layout

One basic consideration is the layout of the workshop. Most power tools and large pieces of equipment are pushed against the outer walls so that the central area is as open as possible. Unfortunately, the tools are often positioned so that the machine is open on the right side and partially blocked on the left. This tends to block free movement of the left arm, restricting left-handers' mobility. Moving machines out a little from a wall or corner, or orienting some of them so that the left side is not blocked, will increase the safety for left-handed users without affecting the right-handers.

The clockwise bias of tools

One left-handed trait particularly relevant here concerns screwing or turning components or knobs. Left-handers have far more power, control and comfort when turning in an anticlockwise direction, right-handers' clockwise. This has implications when using machinery controls, as the speed and power dials traditionally increase clockwise. Screws are also designed to screw in clockwise. So a left-hander is naturally more likely to turn equipment down instead of up, and has less strength and purchase when screwing than when unscrewing a screw.

Left-handers usually line up equipment using their left hand and left eye, so for accuracy and safety they need to be comfortably positioned to do so at *all* equipment. Using the weaker hand/eye can lead to poor grip and positioning, and is awkward and *dangerous*.

Safety systems

Safety cut-off switches are designed to be easily accessible in an emergency. This invariably means that the best place for a right-handed user is the worst place for a left-hander to reach. In an emergency there is no time to think: instinct takes over, and everyone's natural reaction is to reach out with the more dominant and accurate hand. Left-handers need to be able to activate all safety systems quickly and accurately before using any equipment unattended. If not, machines should be modified to include an additional safety switch for left-handers to reach.

Handles

To raise and lower handles on equipment such as on a drill press, left-handers have to cross their arm over their body, obscuring their field of vision and adopting an awkward position. Equipment such as this can easily be modified by adding an additional handle on the left within easy reach of left-handed users.

Saws

Saw blades are particularly bad for left-handers. A band saw, for example, opens to the right for maximum freedom of movement for a right-handers' dominant hand. The left-hand side is blocked by the upright, and left-handers are forced to bring the left hand across to hold the wood, bringing their hand directly in line with the saw blade.

Portable power tools

Some manufacturers have now adapted their power tools to position safety overrides at the top back of the hand grip, where neither left- nor right-handers would inadvertently push it on when using the tool. A switch to the left of the handle would be well away from a right-handed user but would be automatically turned on when a left-hander grips the equipment. It would be good safety policy for schools to research manufacturers and only purchase power tools with comfortable ergonomic grips and safety switches positioned for both left- and right-handers' safety.

Unfortunately, some tools are *not* easily adapted. Electric saws have the blade positioned to one side of the motor, which effectively shields the right-handed user from the blade. A left-handed user has the rotating blade directly against the left side of the body.

Circular saws or jigsaws are usually designed so that sawdust is expelled to the left of the cutting blade – directly where a left-handed, left-eyed user will be standing to accurately line up the blade and hold and operate the machine with a steady, dominant hand. Safety goggles must always be worn, and when left-handers are using saws like this, they must be aware of the outpouring of sawdust and have enough room to move out of the way while maintaining full control of the equipment. Otherwise, it may be inadvisable for a left-hander to use it.

Controls should be away from the left-hander's grip.

Teachers' checks

Teachers should show left-handed students the safest and most comfortable method of adapting power tools and equipment to meet their needs, and remain in close proximity, so that if necessary they can reach the safety cut-off switch for the student. They should *not* leave them unattended to 'work it out for themselves'.

Not all left-handers are the same, and a teacher should consult each left-hander individually to find out which side of the blade each student has to look (based on their dominant eye) to line up the blade with the cutting line accurately. This will determine the position of their body over the equipment, which in turn will determine how securely, steadily and accurately they can grip and guide the equipment.

Strongly left-handed students should never be instructed to work equipment with their right hand, or to reposition themselves so only the subordinate eye can line up the blade, as this could be extremely dangerous. Only the individual can judge whether the level of control is as great when using the right hand or eye as the left.

Sport

Advantage left-handers!

It is often stated that sport is a prime example of left-handers' superiority, and certainly some real sporting legends have been left dominant in their chosen sport. So what are the reasons behind this theory?

A processing advantage

The 'leftie advantage' seems to emerge particularly in sports demanding rapid reactions and good spatial judgement. Over the years, left-handed players have accounted for a far higher proportion of world-class champions than would be expected in sports such as fencing, tennis and table tennis. Left-handers also enjoy higher than average success in boxing, squash, baseball and cricket, and perhaps as much as a third of elite fencers are left-handed. The Italian fencer Edoardo Mangiarotti won his first Olympic gold in 1936 and his last in 1960, and his total of 39 medals at Olympic and world championships makes him the most successful fencer in world history. Mangiarotti was naturally right-handed but was forced by his father to fence with his left hand as it was thought to be an advantage.

Nature's fighters?

It has often been suggested that left-handers' advantage in combative sport may provide a clue as to nature's purpose in making a consistent minority of humans left-hand dominant. It has long been thought that, in the days when arguments were resolved by hand-to-hand combat, being left-handed gave a combatant the benefit of surprise against a right-handed opponent. This advantage, however, would only persist if left-handers remain in the minority. Otherwise, right-handers would soon get accustomed to fighting left-handed opponents.

Pelé – famous for his left-footed goal scoring.

A French neuroscientist, Guy Azemar, investigated the proportion of left-handers in world-class championships over several years. During his study for the French Institute of Sport and Physical Education, Azemar became convinced that sporting lefties have an innate advantage, particularly in 'opposition' sports. To explain why, he concentrated on the way the brain is wired up. As we know, the brain consists of two halves (hemispheres) each of which has particular strengths (see page 19), and it is sometimes thought that in left-handers these functions are more evenly distributed between the two sides – left-handed brains are more symmetrical. This means, for example, that in tennis the process of the player seeing the ball coming and actually hitting the ball are both dealt with by the same hemisphere. In a right-hander this visual information has to transfer to the opposite hemisphere to direct the player's movement, adding an extra 20 or 30 milliseconds to the reaction time – hardly significant, you may think, but it can be decisive in world-class sport.

A recent study conducted by scientists at the Australian National University also found the connection between the two hemispheres of the brain to be faster and more efficient in left-handers and concluded this makes them better at sports and computer games, and activities that involve brain and body performing several different tasks at once – even when they don't involve the hands. Some American researchers think that left-handers may actually possess enlarged right hemispheres, giving them superior spatial skills.

A tactical advantage

Many scientists agree that left-handers could have a sporting advantage, but think it is not simply a question of processing speed, and believe the advantage is more tactical than neurological.

Left-handed bowlers and throwers have the benefit of unfamiliarity and they can bowl at a different angle and move the ball in the opposite direction from their right-handed counterparts. Being able to place the ball where fielders least anticipate it has given left-handed players an outstanding record in world-class cricket (see box, page 110). This advantage is so widely acknowledged that some naturally right-handed cricketers are encouraged to train as left-handed players, and a high proportion (20 per cent) of professional cricketers bowl with their left hand.

The tactical advantages of left-handers are also well established in tennis and squash. Martina Navratilova, generally considered to be one of the greatest female tennis players, once pointed out that many players have pet shots such as hitting the ball to their opponent's weaker backhand. Playing this shot against a left-hander will go to the leftie's stronger forehand. A left-hander also has a serve that awkwardly swings away from the backhand of a right-handed opponent.

A psychological advantage

A final big advantage for left-handers in fast sports would seem to be practical: lefties are perfectly used to playing right-handers but for right-handers, a left-handed opponent is a very tricky exception. It might even put right-handers at a psychological disadvantage simply knowing that their opponent will be left-handed and expecting them to have this advantage.

A left-hander bowls from a different angle.

Is the hand quicker than the eye?

In most sports, it is important to encourage bilateral coordination (equal skill with both sides of the body), to develop an all-round capability. In some sports, however, left hand–eye dominance or cross-laterality can be advantageous.

Did you know?

Field hockey cannot be played using a left-handed hockey stick but left-handed players can develop some great shots and tackles that make them excellent hockey players!

Best foot – or hand or eye – forward

An important consideration in sporting handedness is the dominant eye, which may often override the dominant hand in the brain's decision as to which side of the body to use to catch a ball, shoot an arrow or any other activity where the need to line the eye and the hand up accurately are of great importance. If a person is

A left-dominant gymnast will perform cartwheels and other moves facing the opposite way.

Did you know?

Some left-handed sportsmen are not left-handed writers? Everyone has a dominant eye, ear and foot, and right-handed writers who have a dominant left eye will often catch or throw with the left hand as they find they can line this hand up with their dominant eye more accurately.

cross-lateral (has an opposing dominant hand and eye) they may well choose to catch a ball in their weaker hand, since their spatial judgement is less accurate using their stronger hand.

The many different combinations of dominant eye/hand/foot can have advantages in different sports. Being mixed-handed or equal-footed (equally skilled with both feet) is obviously an advantage in sports such as basketball, American football, soccer and rugby. It is also a plus in hockey, both field and ice, where the player needs to shift grip rapidly to power a shot from right or left.

Same side, or 'congruent', hand–eye dominance is an asset in racquet sports, such as tennis, squash and badminton. If the dominant eye (which governs our aim) is on the opposite side from the dominant hand, the racquet is out of sight for most of the swing, and thus correction in aim and positioning cannot take place until much later in the swing.

Opposite, or cross-lateral, hand and eye dominance, however, is thought to provide better balance, and so may be an advantage in sports such as gymnastics, running and basketball.

It is not uncommon for left-handed sportsmen to be right-handed writers, and vice versa. Mixed-handers may quite often prefer one hand for fine motor skills and intricate work needing more sensitivity and precision like writing, yet find the greater core strength and power needed in sports in the opposite hand.

The catching hand is governed by the dominant eye.

Your child and sport

Sports require many different talents, so being a poor catcher or an uncoordinated runner doesn't rule out having fun or showing talent at another type of sporting activity. Here are some interesting points relating to some of the most popular sports your child may enjoy.

Left-handed golfers lead with their left hand (the lower hand).

Teaching sport to left-handers

When your child starts any sport, it is always worth mentioning to the coach that she is left-handed, even if it doesn't appear to have any relevance to the sport in question. Often, as children's body dominance develops, so their hand/foot skills increase and it is important the coach is aware of potentially useful skills they may bring to the team.

Playing to strengths

Bearing in mind the differences between strongly left- and mixed-handers, it is important that your child is judged on his own individual merits and capabilities. If he is particularly skilled with his left side, it may be that, in his particular case, the hours of hard work spent focusing on the weaker side would be better spent honing the natural talents of the dominant side. Such decisions should always be dealt with by discussion between the coach, your child and yourself to ensure your child has the opportunity to reach his full potential, and develop skills in a way that feels most natural.

Children who are quite late deciding on hand preference, or are cross-lateral, are quite likely to appear somewhat uncoordinated in their early years. In the majority of cases, there are three things to recommend while your child's hand–eye coordination and physical development gradually catches up with those of their peers: patience, practice and praise!

Let your child experiment with different ball games, sports and activities, and however awkward first attempts might be, aim to make them lots of fun and encourage every opportunity to get your child working both sides of the body on specific tasks, such as throwing a bean bag or ball, kicking, catching (often with both hands to start with), throwing hoops over a target and rolling a ball at skittles.

Left-handers are a great asset in many sports, with two distinct advantages over their right-handed opponents:

- Left-handers are said to be good at judging distances, so speed and accuracy is better.
- Right-handers are disadvantaged when playing a left-handed opponent as they are not used to playing them. For example, in ball games such as tennis, football, cricket, baseball and rounders they hit or kick and return the ball from a different, and, for the opponent an often unexpected, angle.

Coaches take note: give left-handers the proper training, and use them as your secret weapons – it's amazing how many right-handed opponents get disorientated facing a leftie!

Golf

There are far fewer left-handed golfers than there are left-handers in general, and there are a number of reasons for this:

- Many left-handers prefer to play golf right-handed, as it seems more natural to them: they are leading with their left side, left eye and turning anticlockwise.
- Until recently it was difficult to get hold of left-handed golf clubs so lefties were forced to make do with what was available.
- Most instructors and instruction materials are right-handed, reinforcing the belief that this is the 'correct' way to play.

Which way you play golf can have more to do with your eyes than your hands and a number of

Phil Mickelson is a natural right-hander who plays golf left-handed.

right-handed people actually play golf left-handed, so they can lead with their right hand and eye. A lot of famous left-handed golf players are actually right-handed in everything else they do. Two good examples are golfer Mike Weir, who won the US Masters in 2003, and Phil Mickelson, who won in 2004 and 2006.

To determine which is more natural for you, the trick is to look down at a ball and see which way you visualize it leaving your body – that will tell you which side of the ball to stand. If your child

John McEnroe is one of a long line of exceptional left-handed tennis stars.

however, as they are both more practised in fighting right-handed opponents.

As well as the phenomenal Edoardo Mangiarotti (see page 102), other successful and famous leftie fencers include Cécile Argiolas and Laura Flessel-Colovic.

Boxing

'Southpaw' boxers seem to have a clear edge over their right-handed opponents in the ring. This is probably because the fighting stance of a left-hander is unfamiliar and unorthodox, resulting in punches that come from different directions and angles from those a right-hander would use. Also, a southpaw leads with his right foot, which can trip up a right-handed opponent.

Famous leftie boxers include James 'Gentleman Jim' Corbett, Marvin Johnson, Marvin Hagler and Henry Cooper.

Tennis, badminton and squash

As explained on pages 102–103, left-handers are recognized as having tactical advantages in racquet sports. They are also instinctively good at fast power strokes and their serve can be more difficult for a right-hander to return. In badminton, shuttlecocks are usually constructed with their feathers arranged clockwise, which makes them veer slightly to the right, so smashes are not equally easy from right or left of the court.

Don't be surprised if your left-handed child regularly swaps between hands before deciding on her preferred hand for such 'power' sports. Some top-class players even swap hands sometimes, delivering forehands from both sides rather than always opting for a backhand from their right-hand side.

Famous left-handed tennis players include Martina Navratilova, Jimmy Connors, John McEnroe, Greg Rusedski and Goran Ivanisevic.

Table tennis

Right-handers can find left-handers very difficult to play against, as they have a natural side-spin to the forehand shot that is hard to return. Faster reaction times and a good sense of spatial awareness are also important, and these are left-hand fortes.

shows a preference for playing left-handed, there are excellent resources, clubs and training guides now available (see Resources, pages 122–123).

Fencing

In fencing, reaction times are extremely short (between 300 and 400 milliseconds), which appears to be an advantage for left-handers. The main advantage in the sport, however, is that a right-hander's sword-arm is on the same side of the piste as a left-hander's, rather than the usual diagonal arrangement when fighting a right-hander. A right-hander tends not to guard the right-hand side as much, whereas a left-hander will guard against attack from both sides. Two left-handed opponents may be disadvantaged,

Left-handers have a tactical advantage in racquet sports, but may swap hands for power shots.

Gymnastics, dance and skating

Left-handed gymnasts will perform cartwheels facing in the opposite direction, leading with their left foot and placing the left hand on the ground first. (Gym coaches need to know to move to the other side of the body to provide support in training.) In ballet and ice skating, pirouettes, spins and jumps are traditionally made on the right foot, turning clockwise, whereas the natural inclination for a left-hander is to turn or spin anticlockwise, and balance on the left foot. In solo dance this should not present any problems, but in group dance, just being aware of this inclination can be helpful, as it explains why your child spins into everyone else in routines, and often starts on the wrong foot! Practice and concentration will usually redress the balance.

Why a 'southpaw'?

'Southpaw' is a common sporting term for a left-handed player, and though commonly used in boxing, it is actually derived from baseball. Ballparks were traditionally built with the homeplate in the western corner of the field so that the batter can face east, avoiding the glare of the afternoon/evening sun. An arm of a left-handed pitcher facing the batter would be the closest to the south – and so the term 'southpaw' was coined.

Diego Maradona made history with his left foot.

Supremacy on the cricket pitch

For the past 50 years the world record test batting score has been in the hands of lefties. West Indies legend Sir Gary Sobers held the record from 1958 for a mesmerizing 35 years, until Trinidad-born leftie Brian Lara won the admiration of cricket fans worldwide by famously breaking this and another world record in 1994. Lara's position was usurped briefly by another left-hander, Australian Matthew Hayden in 2003, but he regained the title the following year with a phenomenal 400 runs not out.

to *play* left-handed, often with considerable advantage. Players are permitted to play the ball with any part of the stick other than the rounded back. The flat side is always on the 'natural' side for a right-handed person, but a left-hander can play as if they were a conventional player using reverse stick, and in doing so they can generate a lot more power. Also, the way they hold their stick gives them the ability to turn quickly in either direction. It is very rare to see and very difficult to play against! More details and pictures of left-handed hockey playing can be found on the lefthandedchildren website (see Resources, pages 122–123).

In ice hockey there are no such restrictions and the stick is flat on both sides. In fact, there are a high proportion of left-handed shooters, and many goaltenders catch with their left hand, forcing their opponents to shoot left-handed as a result.

Polo

Polo must be played right-handed: left-handed play was ruled out in 1975 for safety reasons as playing from the other side of the horse would endanger horses and players. HRH Prince William, a natural left-hander, is a keen polo player, but has to play the sport right-handed.

In figure skating the direction left-handers prefer (in both spins and jumps) is generally the other way round from other members of any group. This makes it slightly more dangerous, since they are always moving in the opposite direction from the flow of people doing approaches to jumps and spins. Handedness also needs to be considered when choosing a skating partner.

Hockey

There are no left-handed sticks in field hockey, as the heads are flat on one side only, with a rounded back. There is, however, no reason not

Archery

A left-handed archer will hold the bow in the right hand and draw with the left hand to bring the arrow back under the left dominant eye. An archer with a dominant right eye may prefer to shoot right-handed. A left-handed bow has the sight window cut out on the right-hand side when viewed from the face of the bow.

Cricket, baseball and rounders

In these sports, there will always be a flurry of activity when a left-hander comes to bat, as the fielders have to be redistributed to cover parts of the field that a right-handed batsman would not be able to reach.

Left-handed players are highly prized in baseball – the legendary Babe Ruth was a leftie. For hitters, the natural motion of swinging at a pitch gives a left-handed batter momentum running down the line to first base. Left-handed batters also tend to have a better view of the pitch thrown by a right-handed pitcher. A left-handed batter runs a shorter distance to first base than a right-hander, because the initial stance in the batting box is on the right side of the homeplate. Left-handed pitchers and bowlers are also valuable, because they send the ball in from a different angle, and also because they put a reverse spin on the ball. Left-handed baseball gloves are now more readily available.

Football

The fractional time advantage in sight and movement in the brain results in left-footers being slightly faster at getting possession of the ball when racing a right-footer. Left-footers are often equally skilled with their right foot on the ball and thus tactically very important team members, particularly useful on the left side of the pitch in left back or left wing position. The greatest left-footed players are also credited with inspiration and creativity unmatched by their right-handed counterparts.

Famous left-footed football players include Pelé, Michel Platini, Ruud Gullit, Marco van Basten and Diego Maradona.

In football, left-footers can be slightly faster at gaining possession.

Rugby

In rugby, it is customary to put the weaker defensive players on the left – the opposition's right – because fewer balls move this way. It was left-hander Jonny Wilkinson's drop kick that won England its first ever Rugby World Cup against Australia in 2003.

Music

Nurturing individual talents

The playing of music is a wonderful vehicle for creative expression, and any interest in music your child shows should be encouraged and nurtured. You may also find your left-hander has a particular flair for music.

Melody-making

With so many of the essential elements for musicianship located in the right hemisphere, such as harmony, pitch and music memory, pre-motor skills for learning music, creativity and imagination, it is no wonder that left-handers are often considered to be very musical.

Increasingly, researchers are using musical prowess to study the relationship of the two sides of the brain. Complex rhythm is located in the left hemisphere, and a theory has emerged that suggests that mixed-handers, with efficient interaction between the musical centres of the brain, may be better at playing instruments requiring both hands to work together to produce a single melody (such as strings or woodwind) whereas strong right- or left-handers may more readily focus the two hemispheres of their brain on separate tasks, allowing the two hands to work independently (such as playing the drums or piano). For parents, all such theories currently prove is that there are infinite permutations of ability, preference and bias among our left-handed children.

Due to the varying degrees of hand dominance in people, it is important to concentrate on each child's particular requirement, without making generalized assumptions about left-handers' needs, and nowhere is this more true than in music. For many left-handers however, the practicalities of playing a musical instrument can present challenges that their right-handed contemporaries do not have to face, and which their music teacher may not be aware of, or prepared to accommodate. In this chapter we look at some of the most popular musical instruments and explore the various issues you may need to consider.

The violin family

Violin teachers instruct all their students to play right-handed: that is, to hold the bow in the right hand, irrespective of whether they are left- or right-handed, and if you look at any orchestra you will see why. The string players in an orchestra sit together, and one player bowing in the opposite direction would be in serious danger of poking someone's eye out, as well as spoiling the uniform look of the strings section.

The body of a violin, and other instruments in the string family, is designed so that the sound is accessible to the audience when held in the left hand and played in the right, and is structured to support the specific pressure on the strings when played right-handed. For a violin to be left-handed it not only requires restringing in the opposite direction, but for the soundpost and bass bar position to be swapped to face the other way.

Scaling new heights

Ryan Thomson, a string teacher and author of *Playing the Violin and Fiddle Left-handed*, (see Resources, pages 122–123) has documented several amateur left-handed musicians, on violin, guitar and mandolin, who trained to a moderate level of skill in right-handed playing and then purposely took the time and effort needed to relearn to play their instruments left-handed. Not surprisingly, they found that they could actually play better left-handed.

Bowing is a precise skill, so a left-hander may need extra encouragement if learning with their right arm.

As in other areas of your child's life, the degree of handedness plays a part here. The most important aspect to master is the bowing technique, as, like writing, this is a precise skill and is easier with the preferred hand. However, it is probably worth waiting until your child has had a number of lessons in the traditional way before considering the possible need to switch.

When your left-hander is learning right-handed bowing do make sure the teacher knows she is naturally left-handed, and ask that she spend extra time on the fundamentals of the bow arm. The lack of correct instruction can lead to extreme tension, hindering the subtleties of movement in the bow arm, especially for strong left-handers. It is good to remind yourself that bowing is difficult for everyone, whether left- or

right-handed, so do persevere! If, however, after a number of lessons (say ten or so) your child still decides she would rather bow with the left hand, there are 'backwards' violins available (usually at outlets oriented towards folk music, many of which are on the internet). Do check that they have the soundpost and bass bar in the swapped position, not just strung in reverse, before you buy one.

Things to consider:

- Is your child's current teacher prepared or capable of teaching a left-handed violinist? If not, you will have to find another teacher.
- Might your child want to play in an orchestra in later years? A left-handed fiddle is fine for folk or rock music, for playing solo and possibly in a

The recorder is an excellent first instrument for left-handers, as the left hand takes the lead.

Great left-handed musicians who play or played stringed instruments right-handed include Anne-Sophie Mutter, Joseph Silverstein, Nicolò Paganini, Pablo Casals, Thomas Gould and Robert Schumann.

Drums

Drum kits can easily be set up in reverse, with the hi-hat on the right, but many left-handed drummers leave the kit in the right-handed arrangement and just uncross their hands to play. Some instructors teach what is called an 'open-handed' approach, playing the ride cymbal with the right hand and the hi-hat with the left. A child with a strongly dominant left foot may need to rearrange the kit, or buy extra equipment, to operate the bass pedal with the left foot.

Generally speaking, however, drumming is a skill in which both hands are trained to be equally adept, and many drummers prefer to work with a right-handed set-up so that they can sit in and play with other musicians at gigs and jam sessions – it is usually not practical to make everyone wait while you rearrange the drum kit for left-handed playing and swap it back afterwards. It is really down to personal preference, so you and your child should talk it over with the teacher.

Famous left-handed drummers include Phil Collins, Ringo Starr and Ian Paice.

Woodwind and brass

These instruments should not produce any major problems for left-handed players. Both hands have an equal role, with the left traditionally being on top of woodwind instruments. Although the modern flute extends to the right side of the body, this is quite a natural progression for most players who start out on a recorder, whistle or similar instrument, as the left hand is still on top (closest to the blow hole).

The French horn actually shows a left-handed bias, as the right hand is inserted into the bell and the left hand plays the keys.

Piano and keyboard

The two-handed practice required to become a pianist helps musicians to develop excellent

school or community orchestra to a reasonable standard, but if your child wants to pursue violin to a high standard, it is unlikely that a classical orchestra would accept a left-handed violinist. As a soloist however, left-handed playing can set you apart and inject real character into the music.

- Depending on the standard your child has reached, is she prepared to relearn her skills in the other hands? Some left-handers have been able to switch with remarkable ease, but many find it difficult, so be prepared for her to experience some frustration.

If she does decide to persevere with playing the traditional way, here's one encouraging thought – as a leftie playing 'right-handed', just think of what a fantastic left-hand pizzicato she could have!

bilateral skills. Improving the non-dominant side of a new pupil is the starting point for every music teacher, and it is usually very obvious if a new piano pupil is left-handed, because the lower, bass register is played with much greater vigour and confidence than the higher notes, which are played by the right hand, and which more commonly hold the melody of the piece. The right-hand practice needed to match the left in agility, rhythm and subtlety has the added benefit of strengthening bilateral skills, but this may not come easily to your child, so much praise is deserved not just for achievement but for perseverance!

The left-handed piano

Christopher Seed is a professional concert pianist who plays the world's first left-handed piano – a complete and faithful mirror image of a standard piano in every sense, with all parts, including the keyboard and pedals, in reverse.

Already a highly respected and successful classical pianist when he undertook this project, Chris Seed's motivation for creating this unique and fascinating instrument was an instinct he has retained since his first introduction to a piano as a child – that the lower, bass notes should start at the right of the keyboard, and ascend to the higher treble register at the left. Of course this is the opposite direction from conventional keyboards. Quite logically, Chris believes that his left hand, and indeed the whole left side of his body, is much more expressive and agile than his right.

With classic left-handed thinking, Chris questioned the conventions, not of the way music was written, but of how it was interpreted on the keyboard. Who first decreed that the top line of music (traditionally the melody) must be played by the right hand, while playing the bass line (more often the accompaniment and rhythm) must be the designated role of the left hand?

Phil Collins, a left-handed drummer who also sings a bit!

And why must lower notes commence at the left and rise to the right? Most piano music is written with the melody in the right hand supported with chords in the left, but if you turn this around and swap hands it makes much more sense to a left-hander.

When Chris was learning to play, his piano teacher was often frustrated that Chris's very accomplished playing with his left hand was not matched by the ability of his right, on which so much depended. At one point the teacher questioned whether Chris should continue playing the piano at all.

With the determination and perseverance common to left-handers, Chris practised until his right hand was equally skilled, went on to study at the Royal College of Music in London and to forge a successful career as a concert pianist and examiner for the Royal Schools of Music. However, he never lost his innate feeling that it would be more natural to play with the keyboard in reverse, and so in 1997 he commissioned the Dutch firm Poletti & Tuinman to build the world's first left-handed piano. A complete mirror image

of a nineteenth-century fortepiano, the high notes begin on the left and move down in pitch towards the right. The lid opens from the opposite side, and the pedals are reversed. Christopher sits facing the left of the stage, so that his left hand and the lid are towards the audience. Not only does playing more of the melodic and elaborate parts with his dominant hand give him a physical advantage, it is also a more instinctive way of playing for a left-hander.

A piano teacher himself, Chris now produces a MIDI module that makes standard electronic keyboards 'left-handed' and would encourage any left-handed player to try playing in that direction. Far from being confusing, Chris maintains that it is an excellent exercise that frees up the brain and makes the player far more intuitive and adaptable. (At the age of 12, my son, a keen left-handed pianist, tried out an adapted keyboard and within minutes was playing confidently and happily, reading the music as normal and transferring the roles of the left and right hand with ease.)

Guitar

Left-handed guitarists are becoming more and more common. Left-handed guitarists use their right hand to form chords and their left hand to pick or strum the strings, but don't automatically assume that a left-handed writer will prefer to play the guitar this way round. Playing right-handed does mean that the stronger left hand is doing the fretwork (although if this was a huge advantage, all right-handers would fret with their right hand, which of course they don't), but left-handers whose rhythm and precision are far greater in their left hand may well prefer to strum with it. They will probably tell you that strumming right-handed 'just doesn't feel right'.

Give your child a standard or a toy guitar and you will see from the way he holds it whether he prefers to strum with his left or right.

You may find that a guitar teacher will want your child to play right-handed. This is more convenient for the teacher, who may not have taught a left-hander before, and may not want to get involved in getting left-handed chord sheets, instruction books, or of course a left-handed

A left-handed guitarist, like Kurt Cobain, forms the chords with his right hand and strums with his left.

Left-handed guitars are becoming more readily available.

guitar. However, thanks to the internet there is now a wide choice of left-handed acoustic and electric guitars and accoutrements available, right down to left-handed thumbpicks. Prices, which have traditionally been higher, are becoming comparable to right-handed versions, so if your teacher's concern is the time involved in setting up for a left-hander, it may be helpful to volunteer to find the necessary items yourself. Shop around for the best deal.

For a beginner, rather than invest too much in a new instrument straight away, it is possible simply to restring a standard guitar by swapping the following strings:

- First (E treble) and sixth (E bass)
- Second (B) and fifth (A)
- Third (G) and fourth (D).

To 'convert' an acoustic guitar, the nut must be replaced and the saddle slot in the bridge must be filled and recut to correct the saddle angle and intonation. Pickguards, while they can be removed, often leave a very noticeable 'tan line', so many players opt to leave them and simply add another or go without.

Jimi Hendrix

There are many great stories of left-handed guitar players who taught themselves to play a standard guitar *without* restringing it – Jimi Hendrix being a famous example. He turned his guitar round and played the strings upside down. Impressive though this is, it is much harder to do, so your child will probably be better sticking to the more conventional left-handed method!

If your child's teacher is right-handed, the usual handy hint for teaching left-handers applies: to sit opposite, so your child will automatically have a mirror image of the teacher's movements to copy.

For the ultimate guide to left-handed guitarists and guitars, see John Engel's book *Uncommon Sound* (see Resources, pages 122–123). Famous left-handed guitarists include Kurt Cobain, Jimi Hendrix, Paul McCartney and Bob Geldof.

Conclusion

Attitudes and awareness regarding left-handedness have improved tremendously over the past decade, and continue to do so day by day. This is largely due to positive pressure from parents of left-handed children, left-handers themselves increasingly refusing to compromise, and pressure groups such as the Left-Handers' Association highlighting areas needing improvement.

Increasingly teachers, parents, product designers and planners are beginning to take left-handers' needs seriously and we are seeing a slow but gradual move away from the heavily biased designs that seemed to equate 'ergonomic' with 'totally right-handed'. Manufacturers are starting to include left-handed versions of everyday items in their ranges and, crucially, left-handers themselves are realizing the benefits of properly designed equipment, and choosing left-handed versions where possible. The more left-handers continue to question poor design and any unnecessary bias, the less they will have to compromise in their daily lives.

Your left-handed child

Left-handed children are often extremely creative and, with consideration and encouragement from parents and teachers, can learn to overcome many of the obstacles encountered through living in a right-handed world. By removing needless hurdles from their early learning experience, you will give them the confidence to explore the sporting, musical and artistic activities at which they so often excel, and in doing so become far more adaptable, confident and capable at school and beyond.

Learning from experience

Through the years, I have heard from hundreds of parents whose children have avoided various tasks at school, including cutting, handwriting, certain sports and crafts, because they felt they were 'not much good'. Overwhelmingly, the difficulties were due to the wrong equipment, or inadequate guidance in how to adapt skills efficiently for left-hand working. If your child finds new tasks awkward or difficult, help her to question whether there might be a more comfortable and efficient method for working as a left-hander. Try doing the task left-handed yourself to appreciate the problem your child is struggling with, and try and work with your child to come up with a practical solution.

Look out for toys that work properly in the left hand.

Do practical tasks with your child to appreciate what works best for her.

Help teachers to help your child

Ensure teachers are supportive and encouraging in helping with these adaptations. If any teachers are unsure of how to help, I hope the strategies and suggestions in this book will be useful. They can also find the latest advice on left-handed techniques for a variety of subjects in the curriculum at the website for the Left-Handers' Association (see below).

The Left-Handers' Association

The Left-Handers' Association was formed in 1990 to act as a pressure group to increase awareness of left-handers' needs in all areas of daily life. Through its online Left-Handers' Club it offers left-handers worldwide the opportunity to share their experiences and opinions, contribute to regular and wide-ranging studies and to benefit from the experience of a dedicated team of fellow lefties, who are always 'on hand' to offer suggestions and advice on anything from writing challenges to the latest left-handed equipment.

Since its formation the Club has gone from strength to strength with members all over the world and is highly regarded as the foremost pressure group and advice centre on all aspects of left-handedness.

The Left-Handers' Club is completely free to join at www.anythingleft-handed.co.uk and members receive:

- A monthly newsletter by email with reports on the latest research, practical issues, products and successes by famous left-handers
- Membership certificate
- Backwards calendar
- Early access to new left-handed products and regular member discounts

Resources

Further reading: General books about left-handedness

Right Hand, Left Hand Dr Chris McManus, Orion Books (2003)
The Left-hander's Handbook Diane Paul, Robinswood Press (2002)
The Left-handed Book Simon Langford, Anything Left-Handed Ltd (1995)
The Natural Superiority of the Left-Hander James T. de Kay, M. Evans & Co (1979)
A Left-Handed History of the World Ed Wright, Murdoch Books (2007)

Books and workbooks for handwriting

Left Hand Writing Skills Mark and Heather Stewart, Robinswood Press (2005)
This book is the first ever range of handwriting teaching and practice workbooks specifically for left-handed children. The series guides children with friendly, entertaining and beautifully illustrated instructions and exercises, helping them overcome the common difficulties of left-handed letter formation to achieve a clear, comfortable writing style. Available as three separate workbooks, a complete photocopiable school's edition or a colour multi-user CD-rom.

Writing Left-handed: Write in, not left out Gwen Dornan, The National Handwriting Association (2007)
This book is ideal for anyone who is helping a left-hander to learn to write. It gives parents and teachers an understanding of the process of writing left-handed, with plenty of practical help, tips and strategies.

The Handwriting Pocketbook Julie Bennett, Teachers' Pocketbooks (2007)
A pocket-sized guide to handwriting for teachers containing useful tips on teaching left-handers.

Craft and leisure books

Crochet Unravelled Claire Bojczuk, Pottage Publishing (2005)
Left-handed Sewing Sally Cowan, Dover Books (1993)
The New Drawing on the Right Side of the Brain Betty Edwards, HarperCollins (2001)
On the Other Hand Steve Anderson, Saron Press (2001)
Mind Maps for Kids Tony Buzan, HarperCollins (2003)
Left-Handed Guitar, The Complete Method, Book and CD Troy Stetina, Hal Leonard (1998)
Uncommon Sound John Engel, Leftfield Ventures (2006)
Playing Violin and Fiddle Left-handed Ryan Thomson, Captain Fiddle Publications (2003)

Stockists of practical implements

www.anythingleft-handed.co.uk
This website features a huge selection of left-handed products for children and adults, including:

- Ergonomic pens with specifically moulded grips or offset nib sections
- Tri-grip pencils
- Cartridge pens and smudge-free fibre-tip pens, rulers, sharpeners and stationery items
- Left Write writing mat, practice and instruction books, training DVD

- Computer mice and keyboards, golf clubs, guitars
- Scissors, craft knives, can openers, peelers and other household implements
- Online training videos on using left-handed scissors, and writing left-handed
- Free membership of the Left-Handers' Club

www.lefthandedguitars.co.uk
A wide range of left-handed guitars and accessories.

www.leftysguitarswapshop.com
Buy, sell or swap left-handed guitars.

www.lefthandedgolf.co.uk
Equipment and advice for left-handed golfers.

Information and advice

www.lefthandedchildren.org
Everything you'll need to help left-handed children from nursery right through their school days to overcome the annoyances and frustrations of living in a right-handed world.

www.lefthandersday.com
Left-Handers' Day is on 13 August each year. The official site celebrates sinistrality, with fascinating facts, quizzes and games focusing on the positive aspects of being left-handed. Free membership of the Left-Handers' Club is available with fun posters to download.

www.lefthandedchildren.org/swapmouse.htm
Free software to reverse the computer mouse button so that it can be used on the left.

www.planetfieldhockey.com/PFH/Item-View-1743
Field hockey shots and tactics for left-handers.

www.lefthandedpiano.co.uk
Details of Christopher Seed and his left-handed piano. The website also provides information on the Keyboard Mirror – a plug-in module that converts your electronic keyboard to a 'lefthand' arrangement.

www.lefthander-consulting.org
Professor Johanna Barbara Sattler, German psychologist and author of studies into changed handedness in children.

Surveys and results on left-handedness

www.lefthandedchildren.org/school-survey-results.htm
Left-handers' school experiences survey.

www.lefthandersday.com
Find out how to take part in surveys on left-handedness including the following subjects: support in schools; family trends; difficulties and advantages; jobs and hobbies. You can also see the results so far.

Index

Page numbers in *italics* refer to illustrations

Acknowlegements

With thanks to Professor Johanna Barbara Sattler and Christopher Seed for the enjoyable discussions and insight into different aspects of left-handedness which we shared in Luxembourg.

Most of all, a huge thank you to my husband Keith for encouraging me to write this book and for his support, patience and guidance in helping me break down such a big project into manageable pieces.

Executive Editor Jane McIntosh
Editor Emma Pattison/Kerenza Swift
Design Manager Tokiko Morishima
Designer Peter Gerrish
Production Controller Nigel Reed

Commissioned Photography

© **Octopus Publishing Group Limited/** Russell Sadur

Other Photography

Action Plus 103.
Alamy/Charles Mistral 116.
Bridgeman Art Library/Louvre, Paris, France, Giraudon15.
Corbis UK Ltd 76; /Ethan Miller 14 bottom right; /Heide Benser 36; /Kevin Cozad 8; /LWA-Dann Tardif 88; /Michael Kim 15 bottom left.
Getty Images 108; /AFP 102; /Charlie Schuck 22; /Frank Micelotta/Stringer 118; /John Giustina 78; /Michael Wildsmith 80; /Steve Powell 110; /Streeter Lecka 107; /Terry O'Neill 117; /Yellow Dog Productions 97.
Masterfile/Gail Mooney 115; /Kevin Dodge 100.
Octopus Publishing Group Limited/ Adrian Pope 45; /Peter Pugh-Cook 62 left; /Vanessa Davies 12.
Rex Features/JG/TS/Keystone USA 14 top right.